# CALIFORNIA
# 2021

by the 4th grade
artists of LFCSA

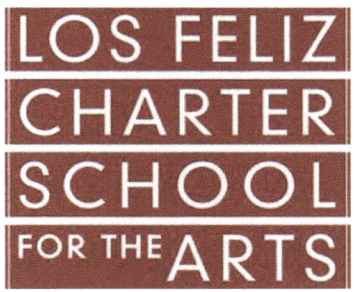

LOS FELIZ
CHARTER
SCHOOL
FOR THE ARTS

## ABOUT THIS BOOK

2021 has been a historic year for our world, our country and our state. Our 4th grade students have demonstrated immense resilience and creativity as we all worked together to overcome the challenges of the pandemic, distance learning, and so much more. Through this year of learning, we explored the wonders of our amazing state, and visited its various regions: the mountains, deserts, coast and valleys. We applied our knowledge of photography to capture our state's beauty. We wrote poems inspired by what we saw and experienced in our visits. We hope to inspire others to appreciate the wonders of our state, and to be its stewards.

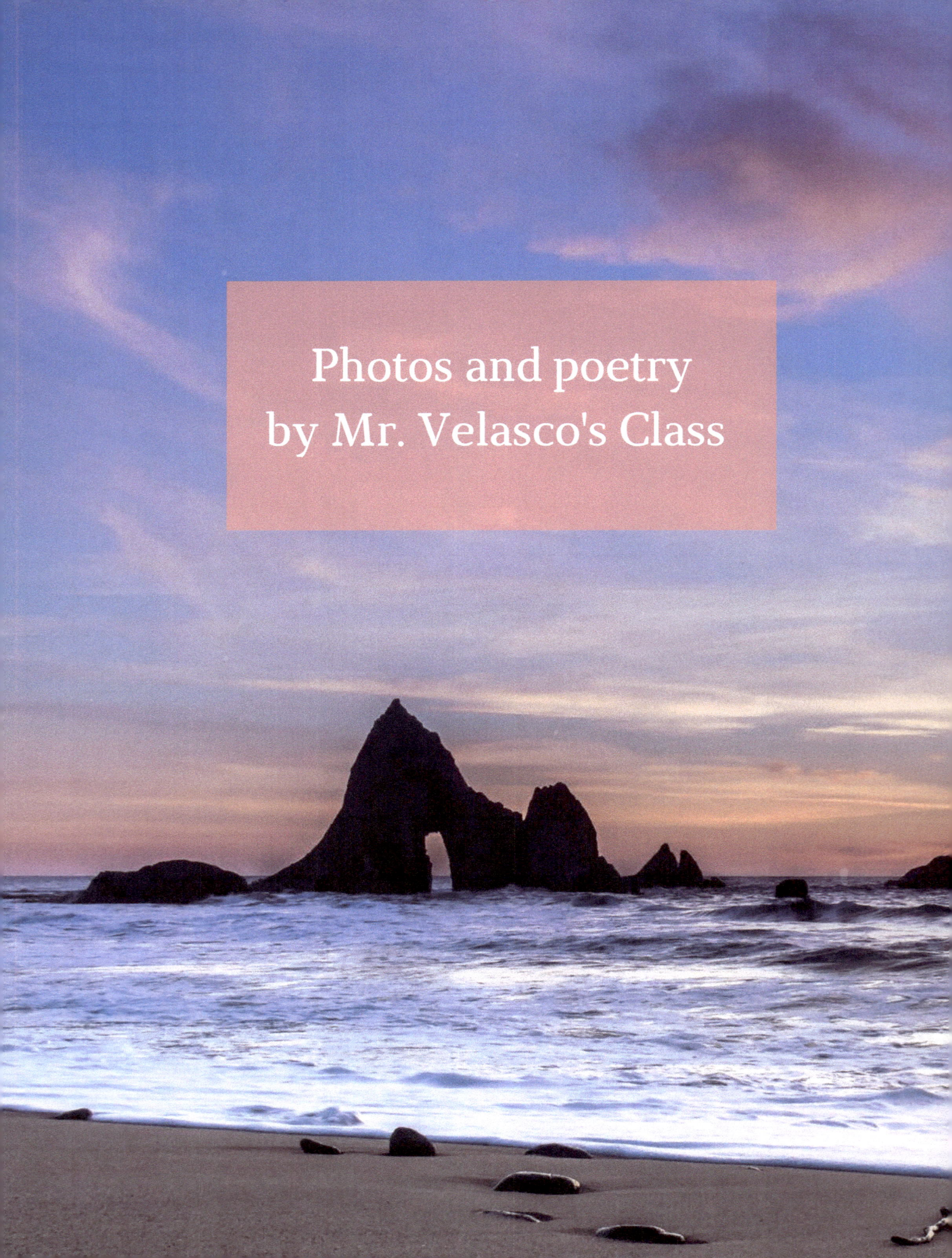

# Photos and poetry
# by Mr. Velasco's Class

# Warm summer sky

It's a warm summer sky with no sounds, no cries.
You are alone with your mind to check in with yourself to make sure you are fine.

By Asher

I WENT
ON A WALK,
I SAW A
LITTLE SMOG
AND A GUY
WITH A DOG,
THEN I KEPT
WALKING
I SAW A
FLYING CROW
AND I NAMED
HIM JOE.

by Caelan

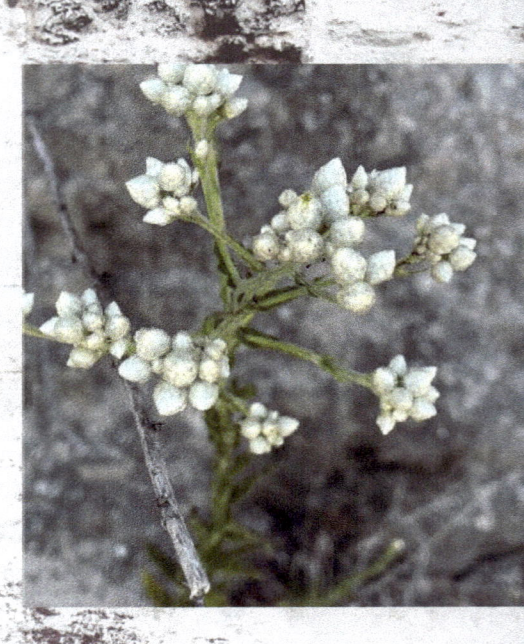
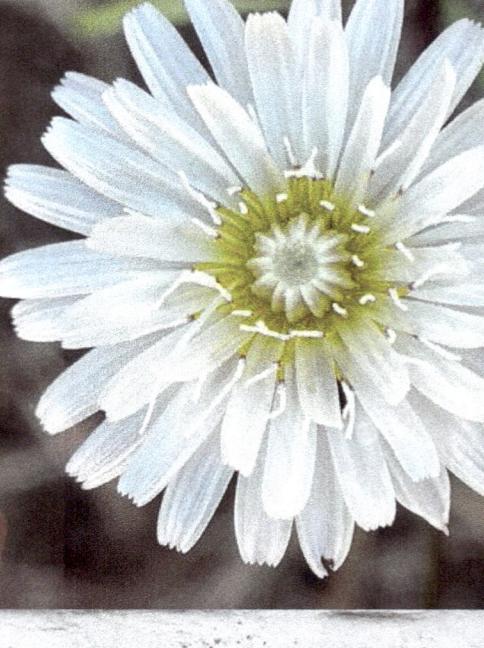
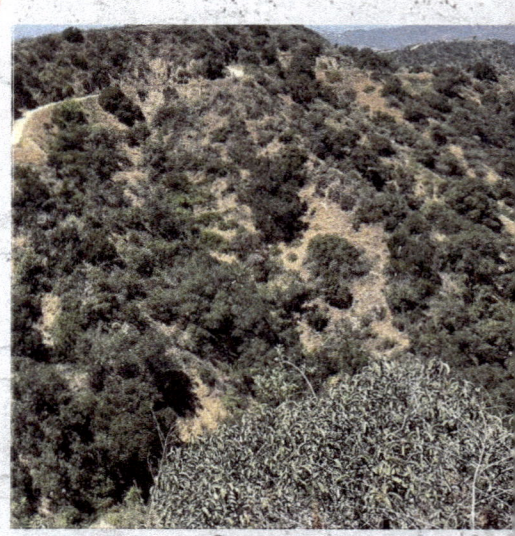

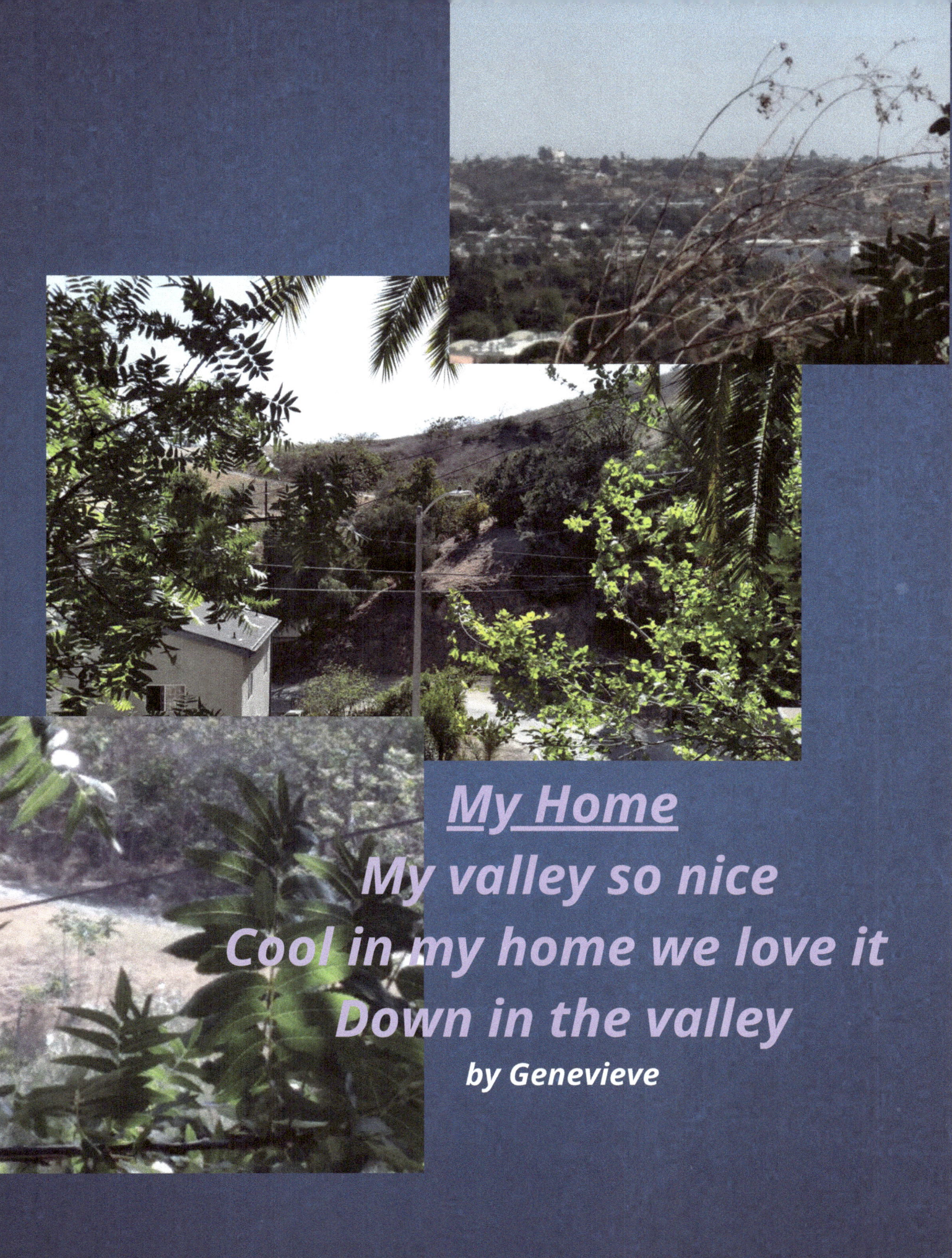

## <u>My Home</u>
My valley so nice
Cool in my home we love it
Down in the valley
by Genevieve

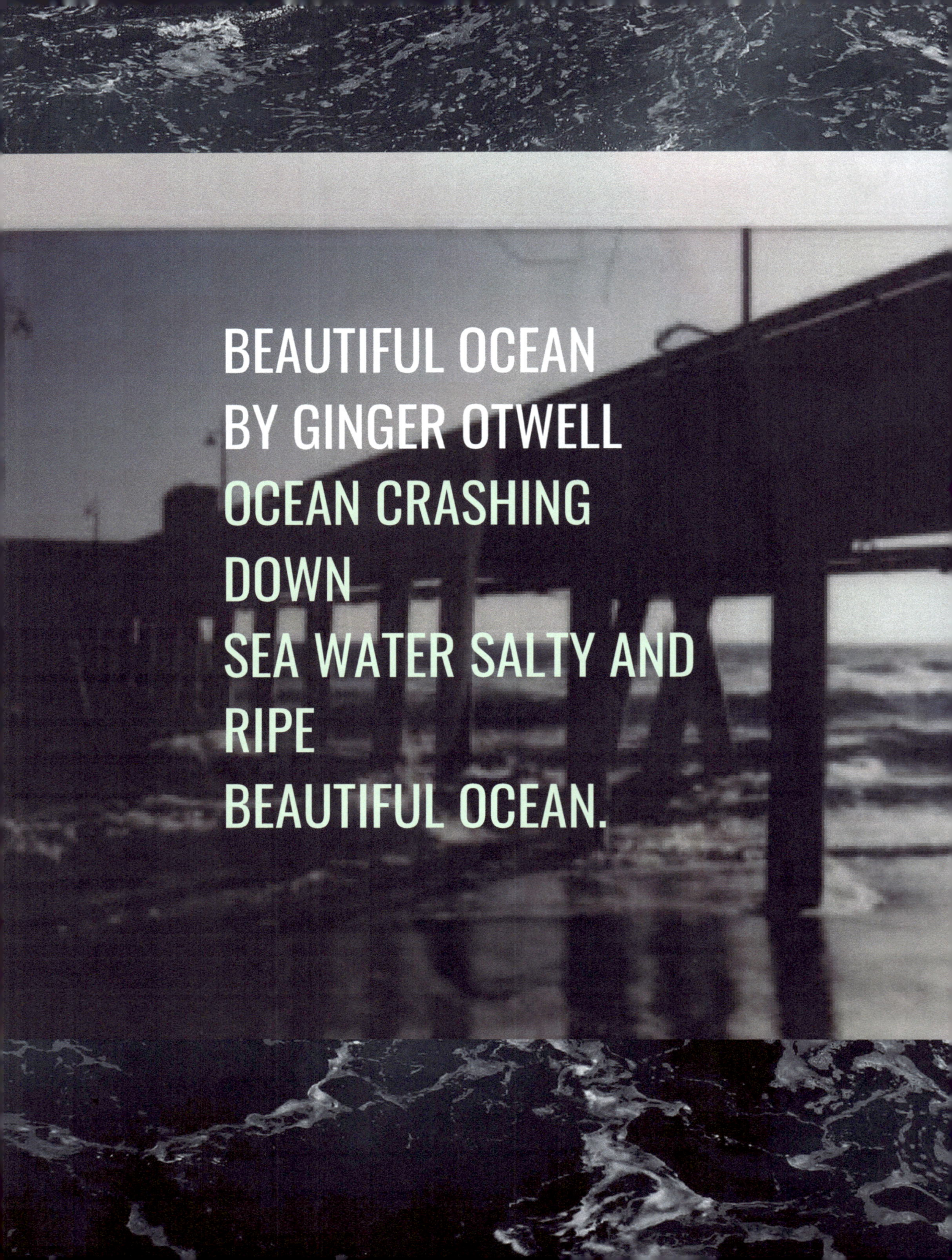

BEAUTIFUL OCEAN
BY GINGER OTWELL

OCEAN CRASHING
DOWN
SEA WATER SALTY AND
RIPE
BEAUTIFUL OCEAN.

# High tide

Big, foamy waves crash.
Sandy feet, salt in the air.
Light on the water.

by Gracie

# harper

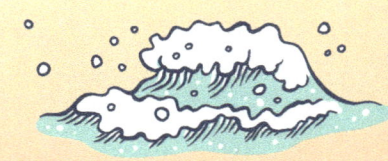

beach fun

cool blue waters
sand in
your toes
waves roaring
and splashing
in the shore

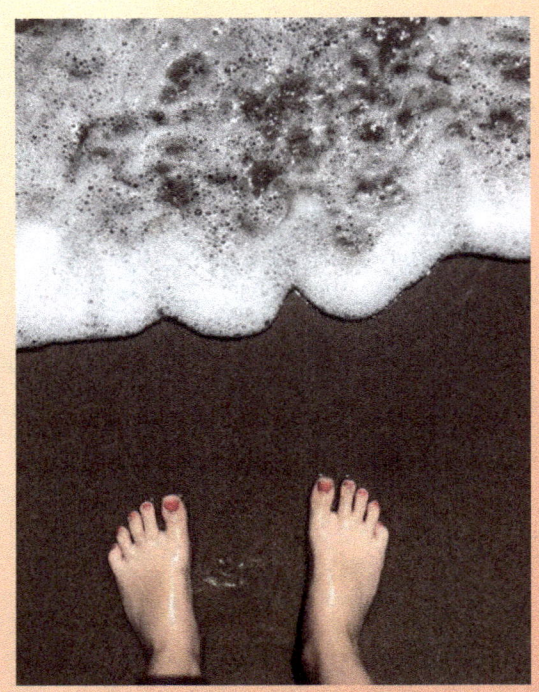

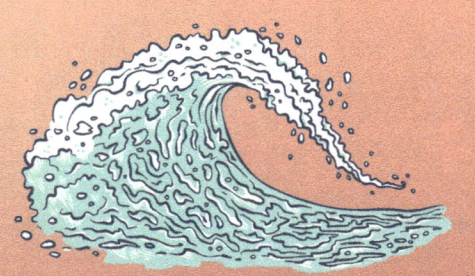

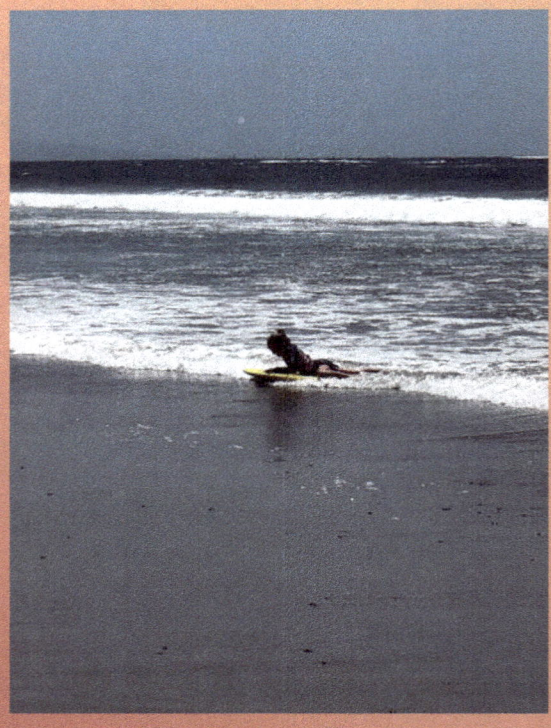

# IZZIE

## BIG SUR

Seals on the hot sand.
Hard rock landforms on the shore.
Fog over the sea.

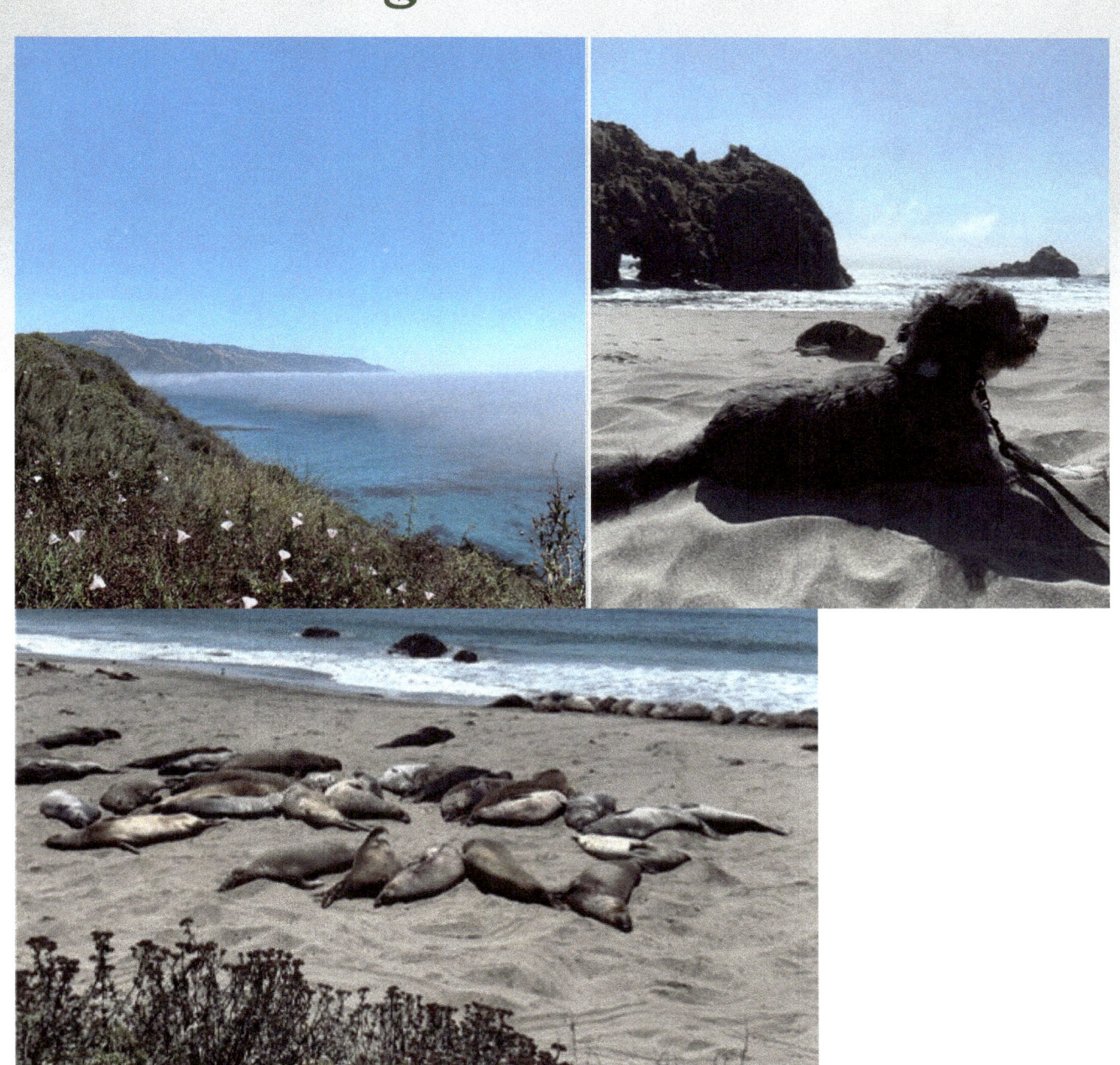

# BEAUTIFUL OCEAN

BEAUTIFUL OCEAN
CRASHING DOWN ON THE SOFT
BEACH
THAT LEAVES FUN BUBBLES

by Jax Kazama

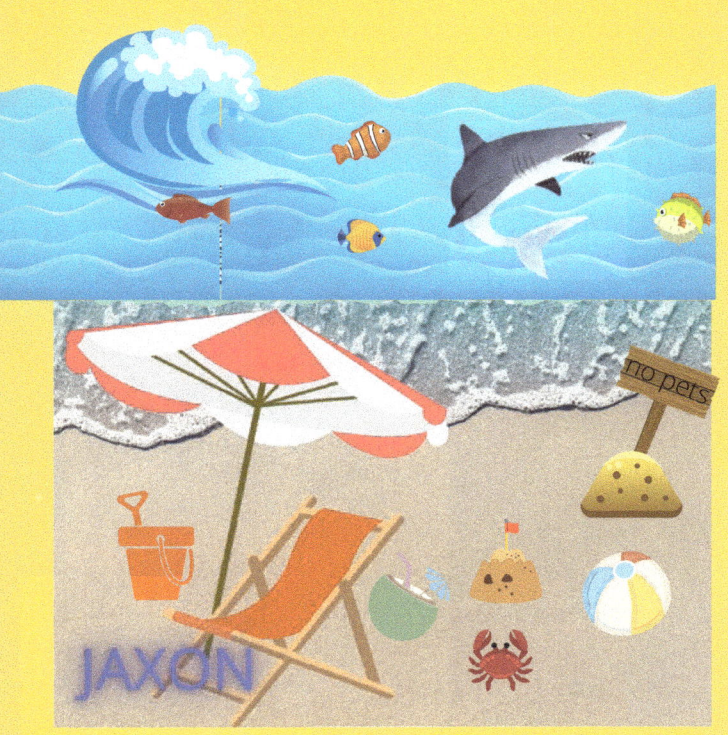

JAXON

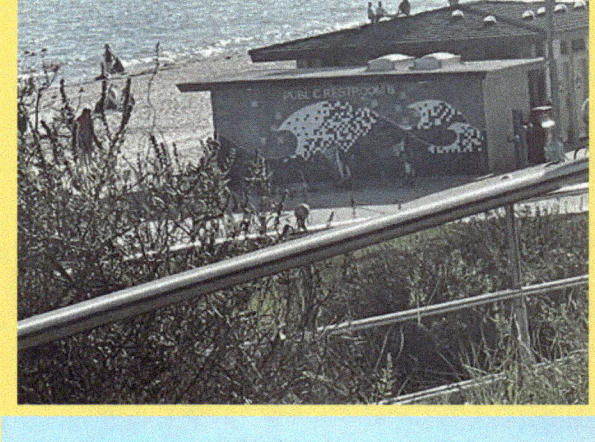

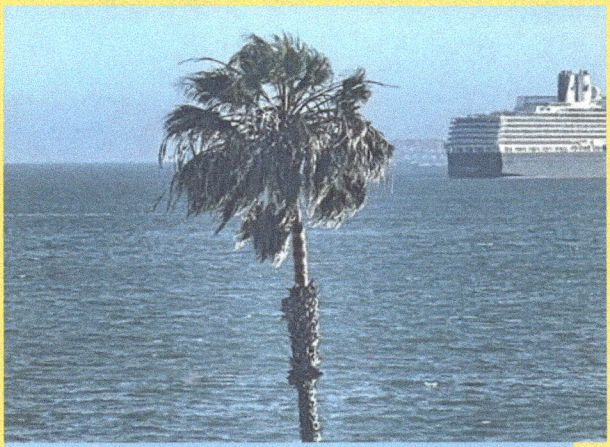

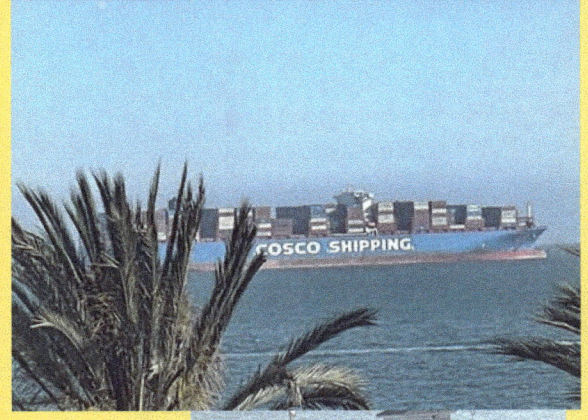

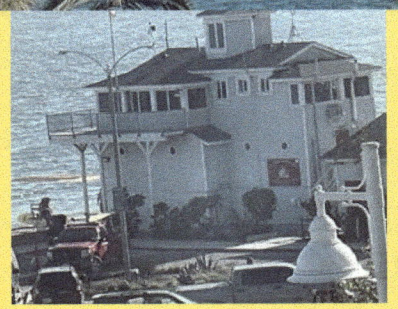

## THE BEACH

THE BEACH IS A BEAUTIFUL PLACE, I LIKE TO PLAY CHASE, THE SAND IN MY TOES SO SANDY, AND HEY LOOK OVER THERE, IT'S SOME MOSS SO GREEN AND SO SOFT, JUST LIKE THAT GLOP THAT YOU GET FOR YOUR LUNCH THAT YOU GET IN COMICS

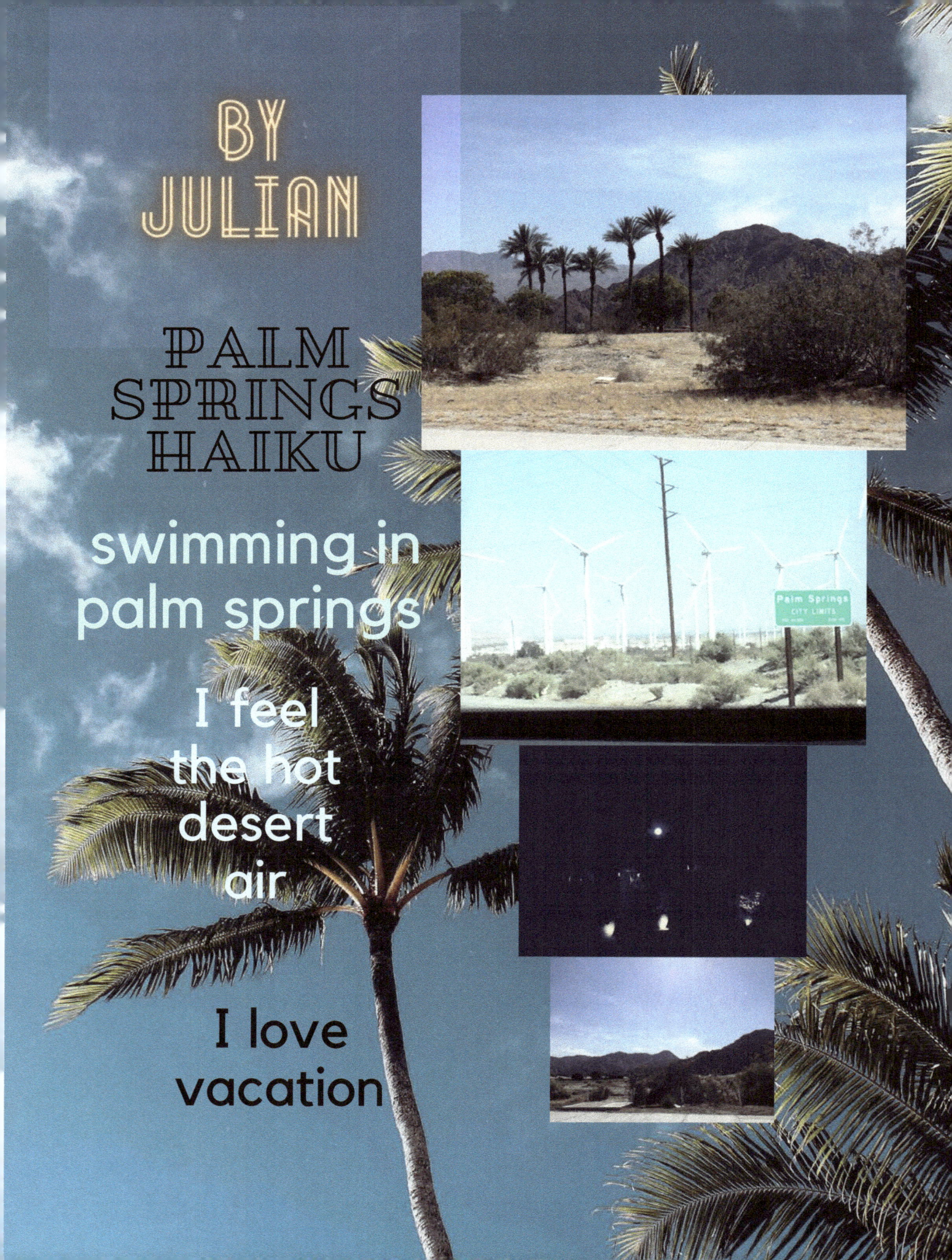

# BY JULIAN

## PALM SPRINGS HAIKU

swimming in
palm springs

I feel
the hot
desert
air

I love
vacation

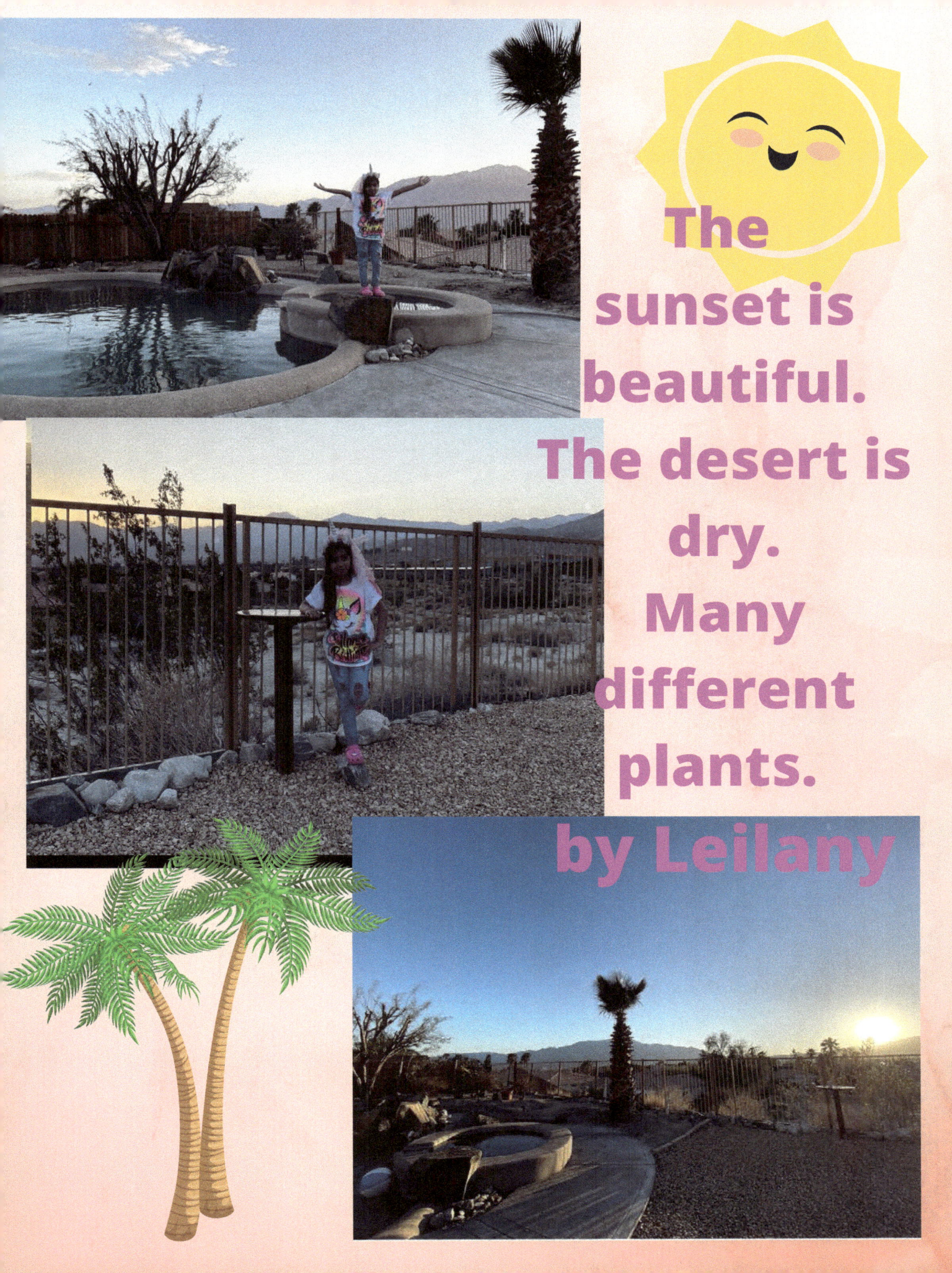

The sunset is beautiful. The desert is dry. Many different plants.

by Leilany

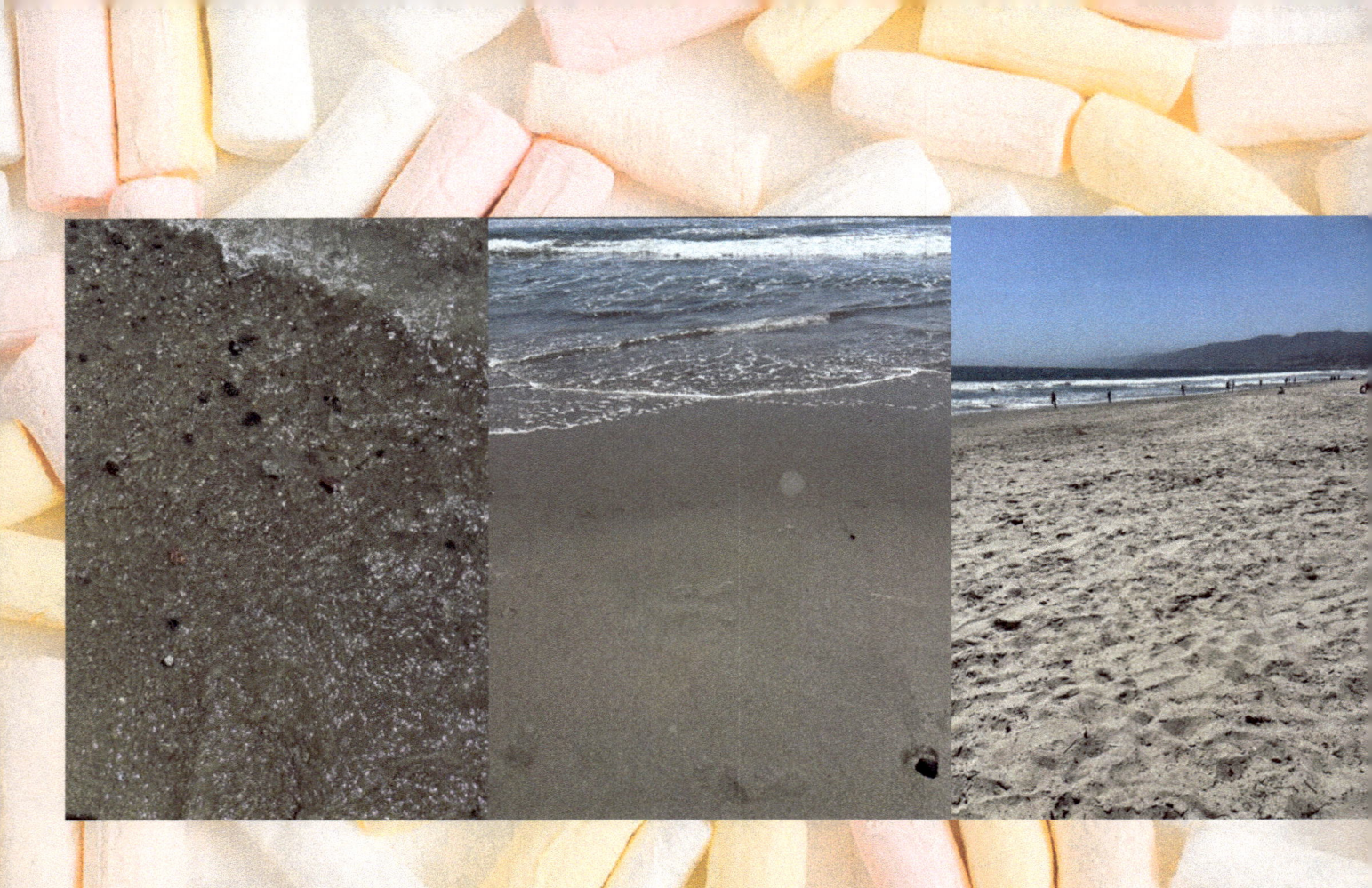

The ocean is like a human
the waves crash against
the shore
it is the way our planet
breathes.

BY MARUSHA

# BY MILO

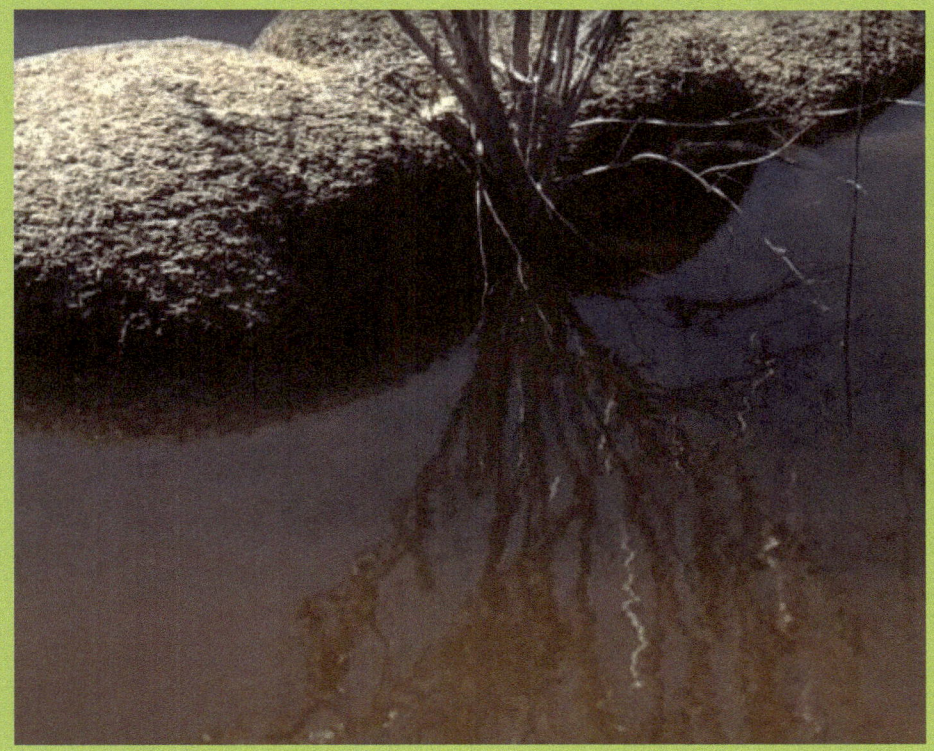

The water is beautiful as the sun the rocks are heavy and smooth and the mountain is the nice part of this...

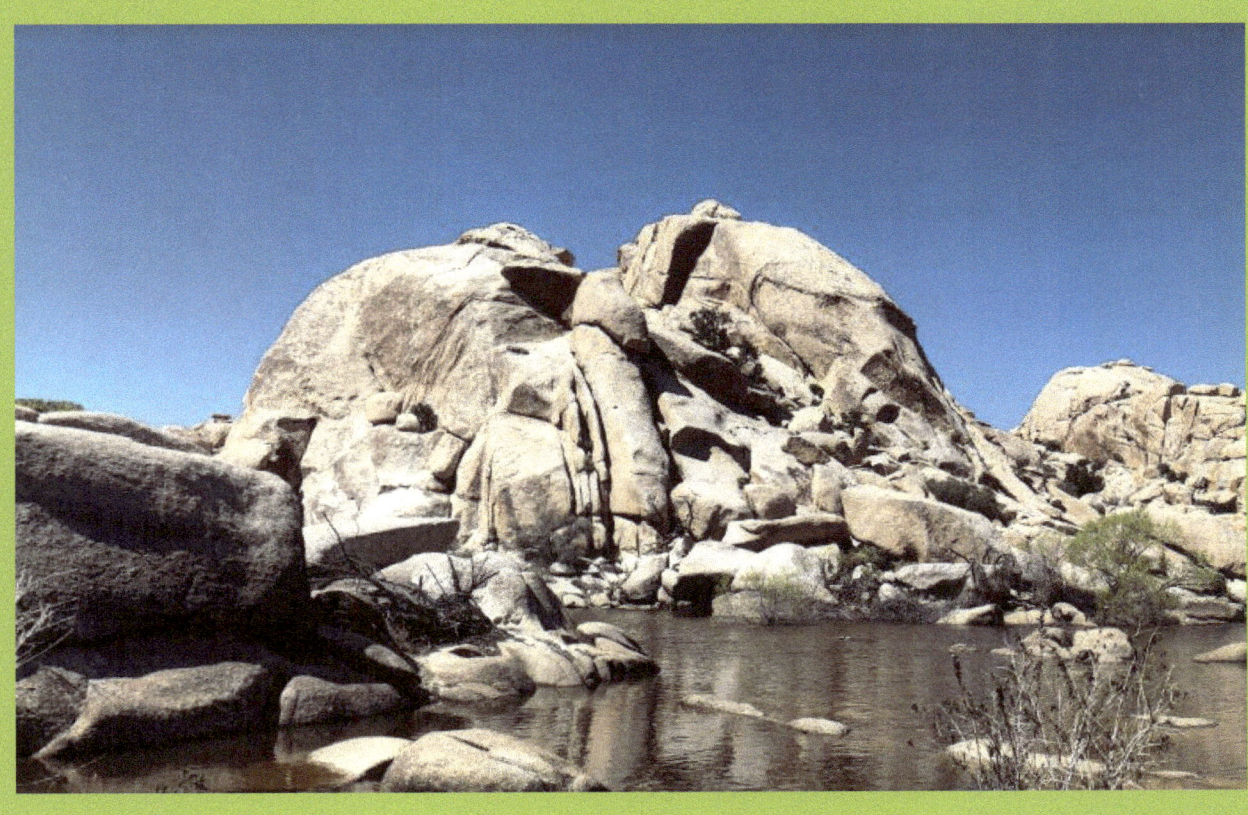

# NICOLAAS

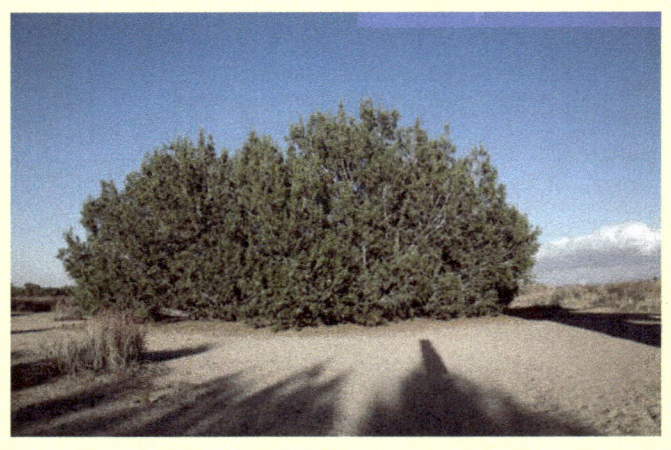

there are junipers
there is wind, spines,
dirt, and me
there is a photo

NICO V. TERRY THE VERY IMPORTANT POET

# MOUNTAINS

## BY NOAH

## THE MOUNTAINS ARE BIG
## SOARING OVER THE GREAT GROUND
## GROWING ON AND ON

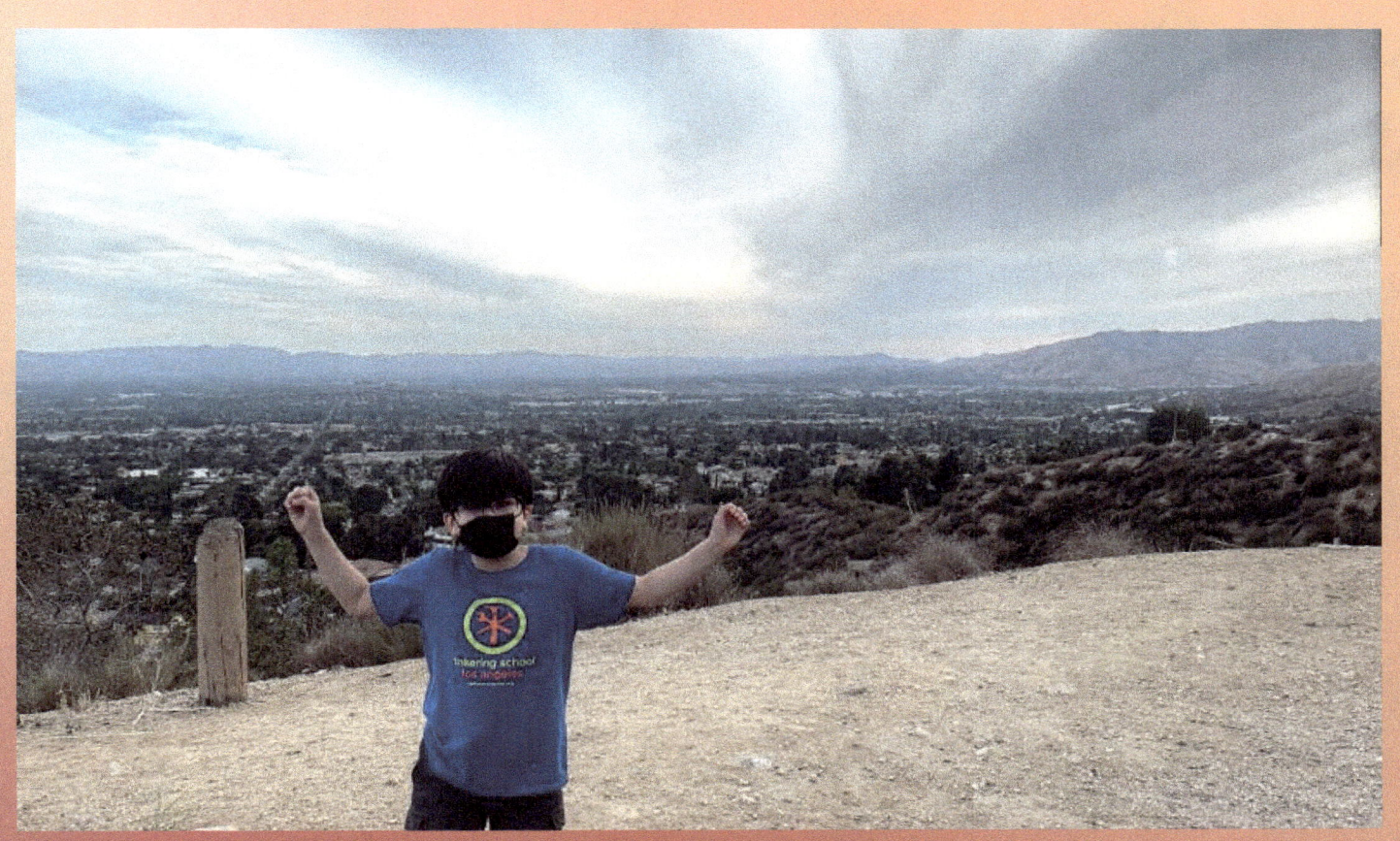

# BY PEAR

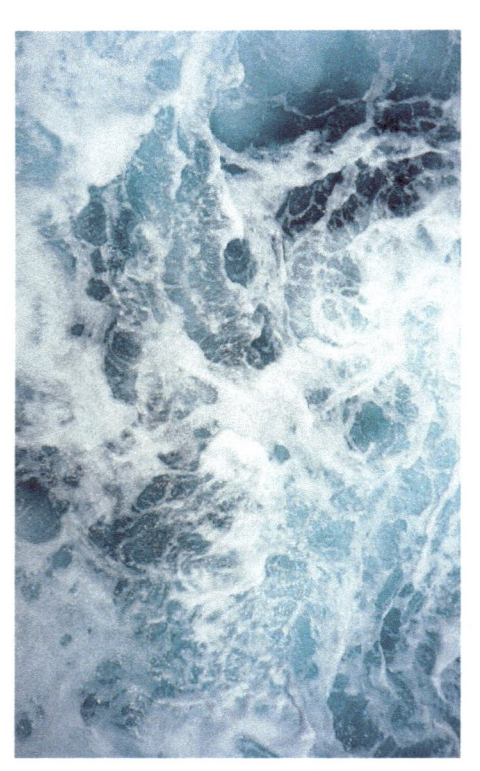 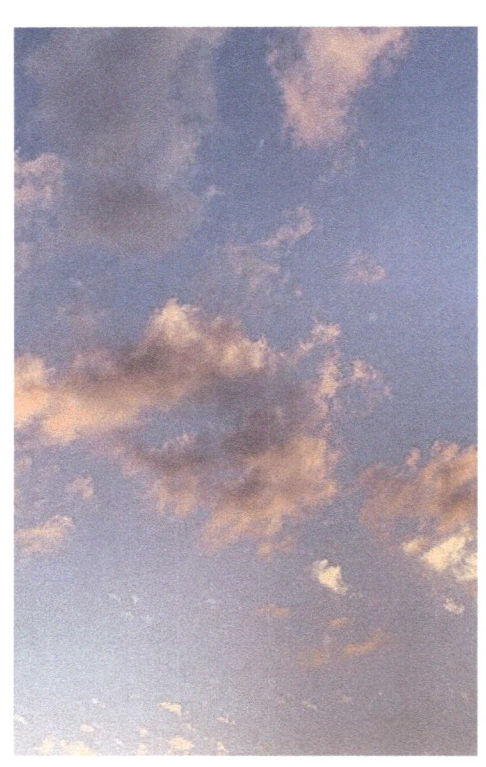 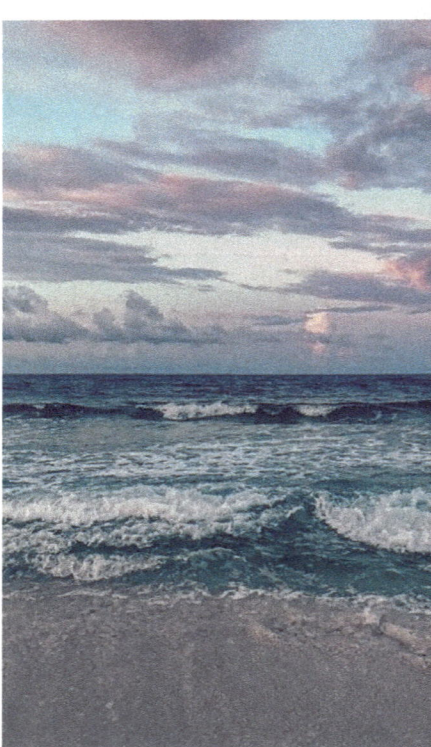

**shimmering waters**
**the waves splashing on the shore**
**cotton candy clouds**

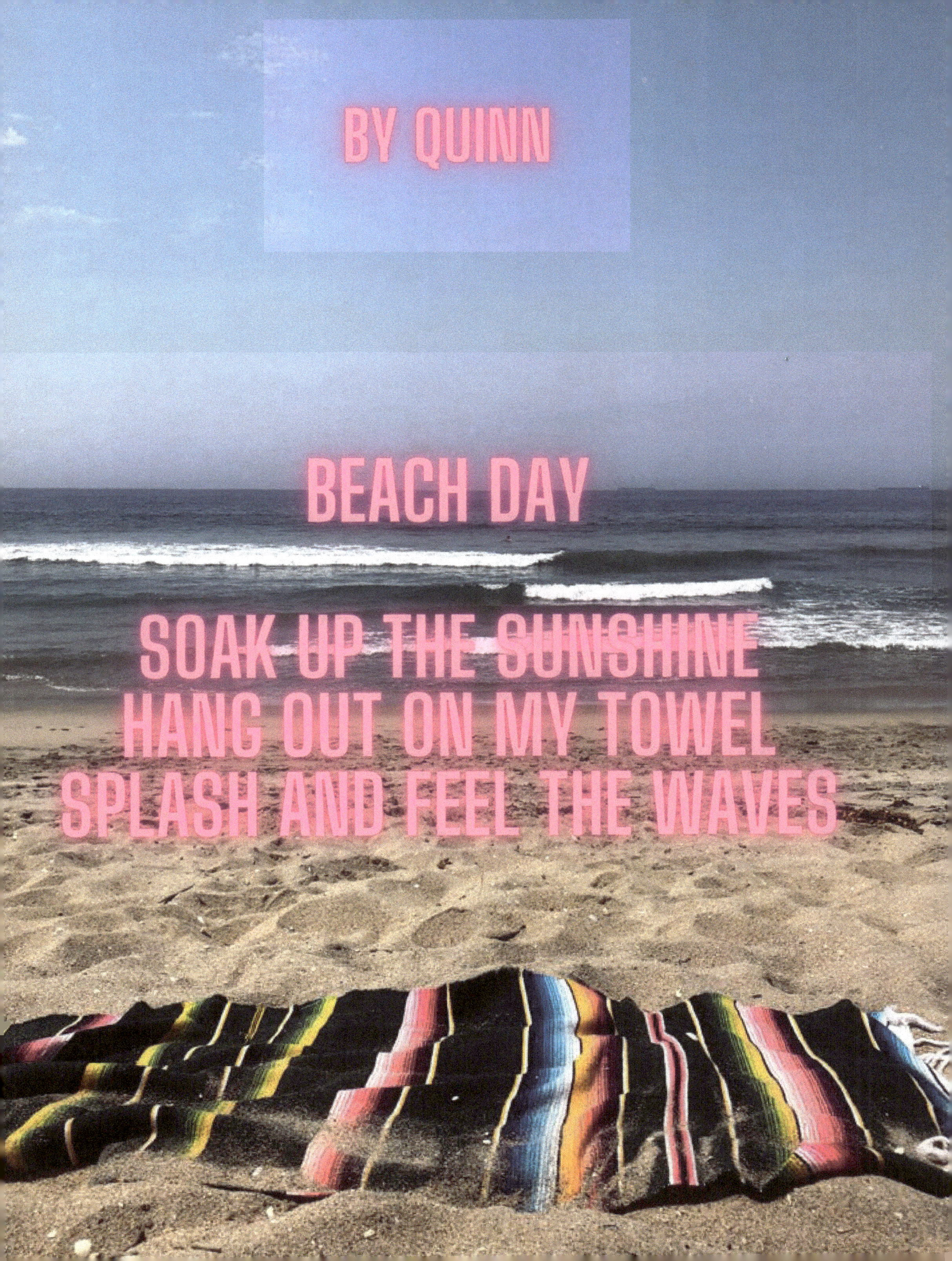

BY QUINN

# BEACH DAY

SOAK UP THE SUNSHINE
HANG OUT ON MY TOWEL
SPLASH AND FEEL THE WAVES

BY RIFF

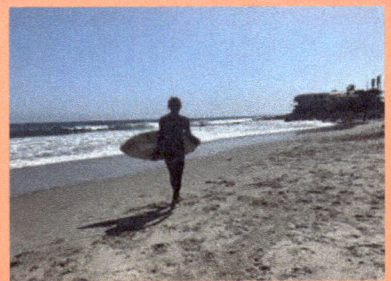

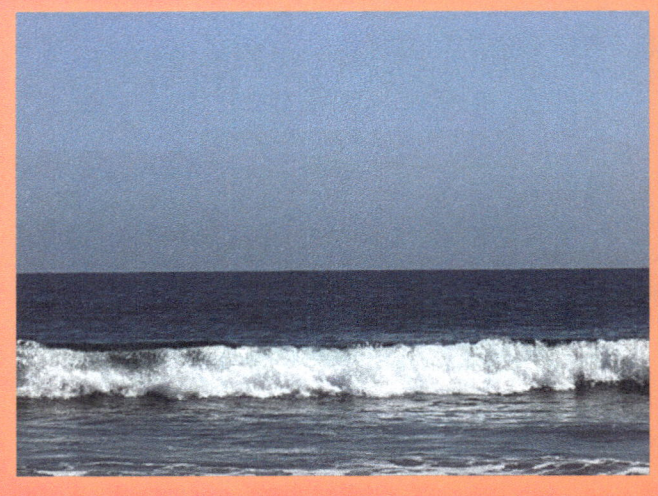

# On The Coast

On the coast, waves crash.
On the coast, shells are sleeping.
On the coast, is love.

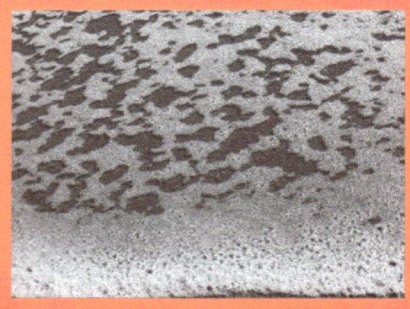

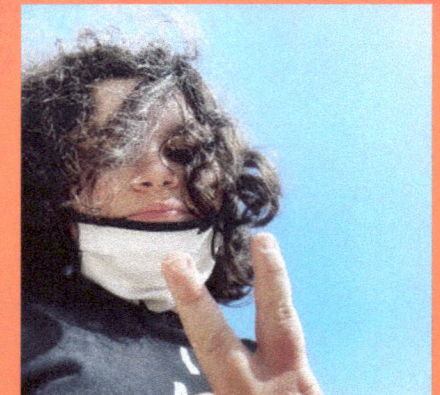

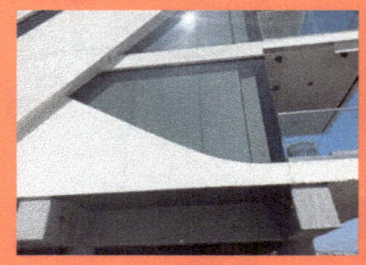

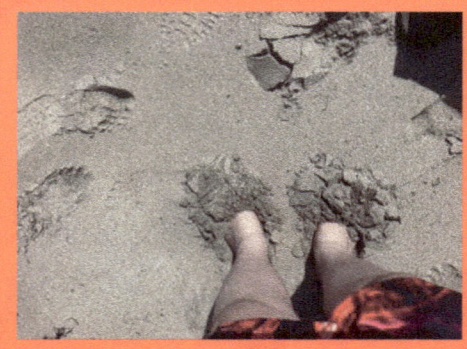

# BY SCARLETT

## an important boat

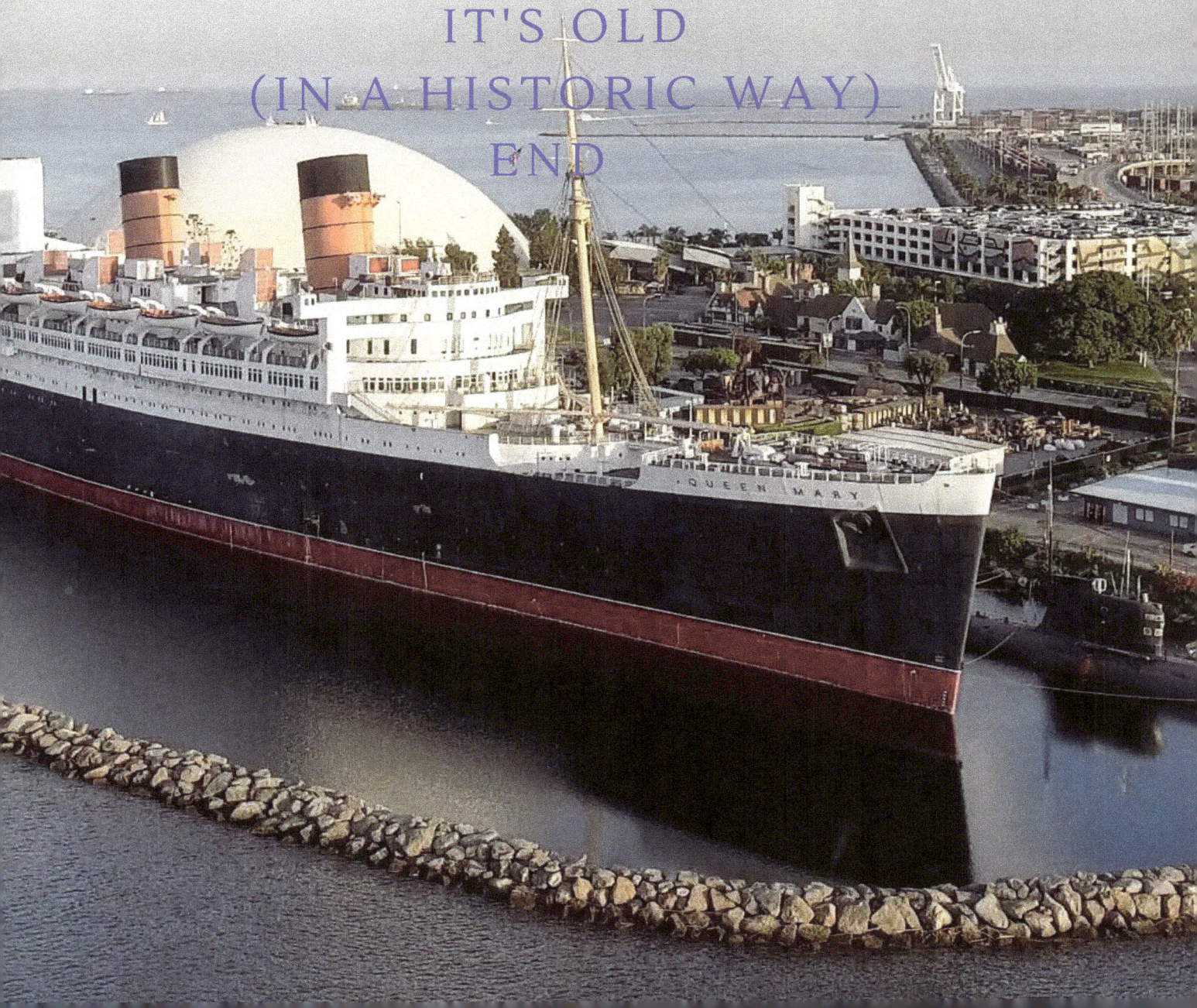

THIS IS A BOAT
IT'S BIGGER THAN A GOAT
IT'S THE QUEEN MARY
IT'S OLD
(IN A HISTORIC WAY)
END

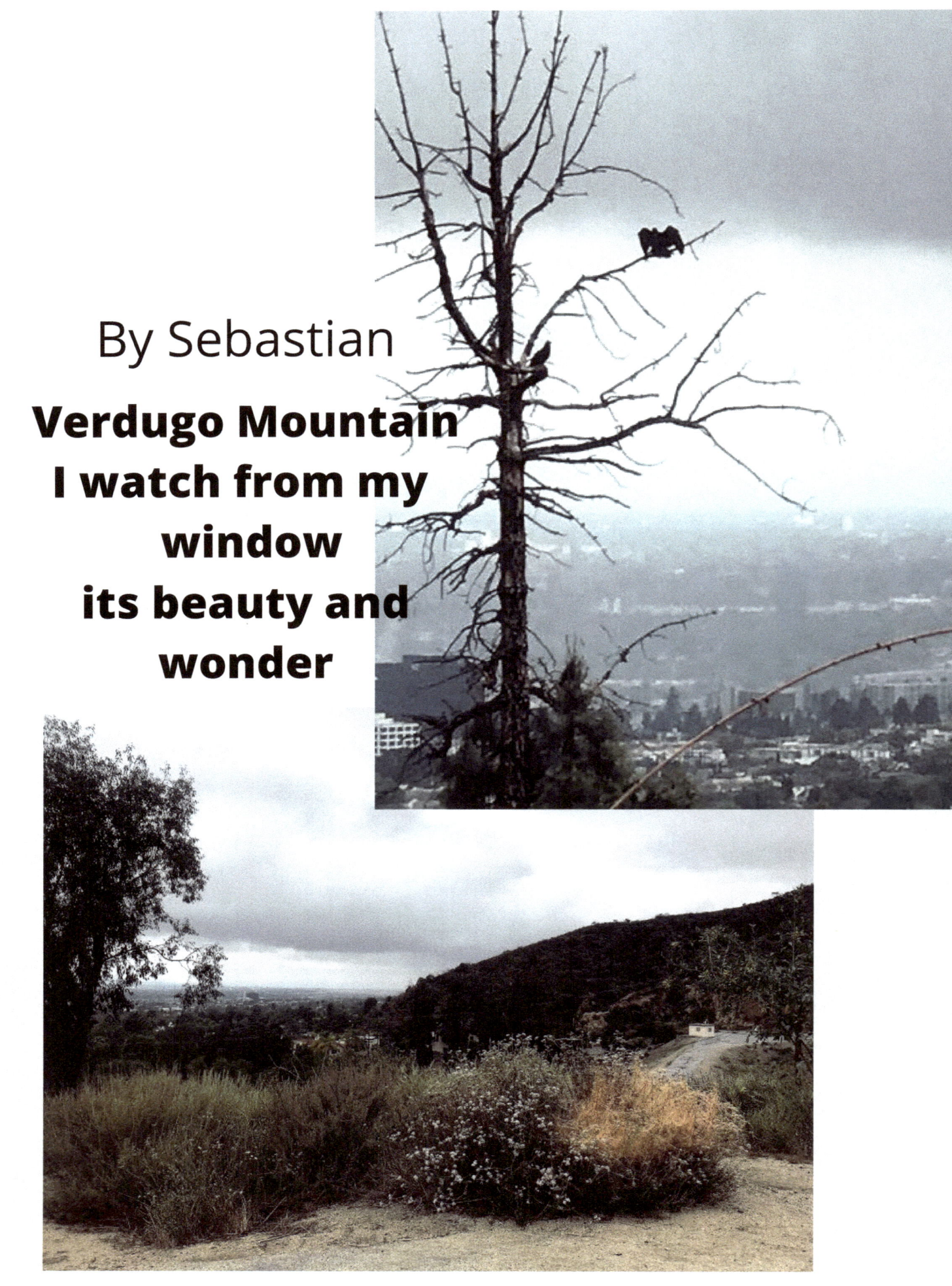

By Sebastian

**Verdugo Mountain
I watch from my
window
its beauty and
wonder**

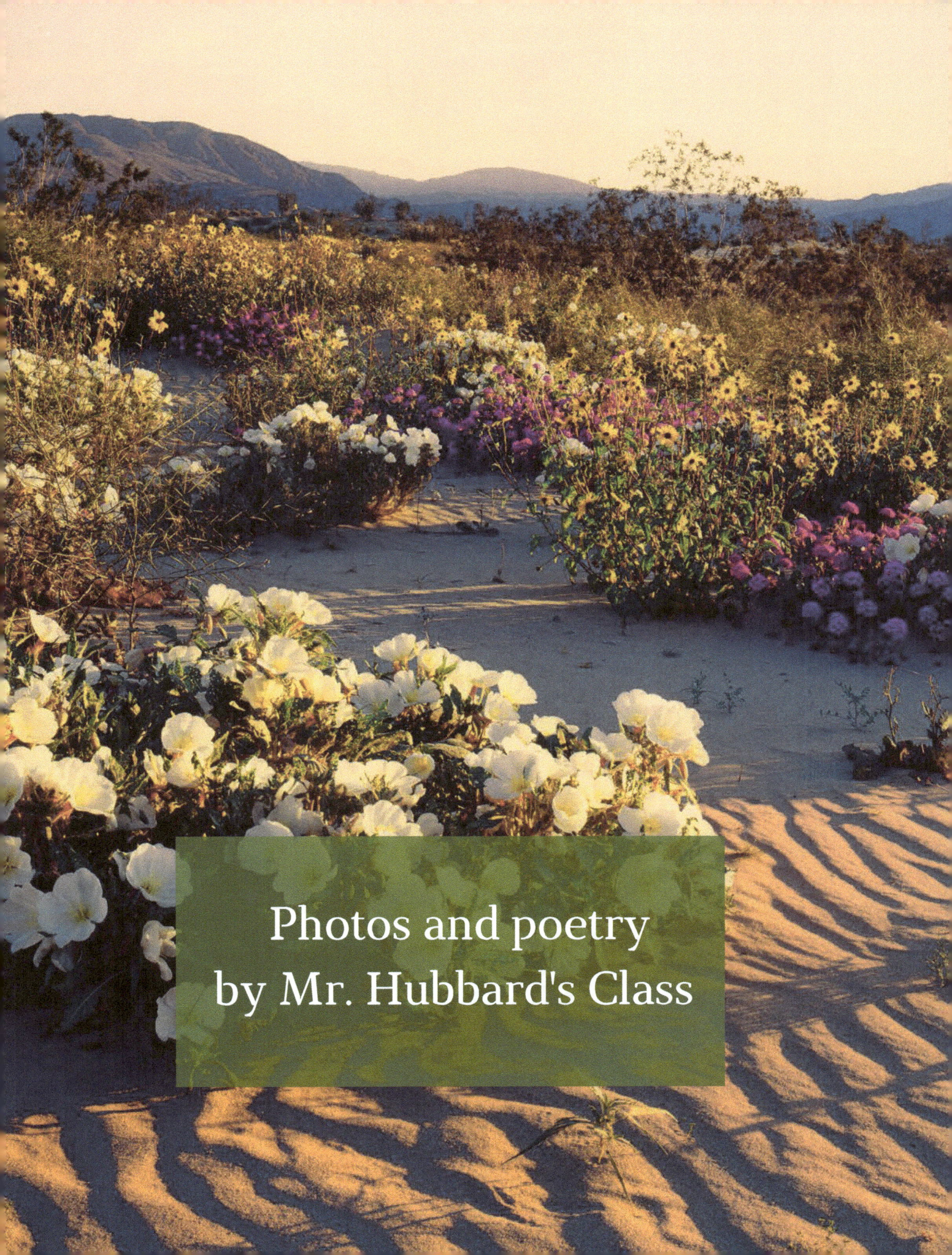

Photos and poetry
by Mr. Hubbard's Class

# By Addie
# THE DESERT

-------------------

The desert is hot

I go there on Thanksgiving

Go to Vasquez Rocks

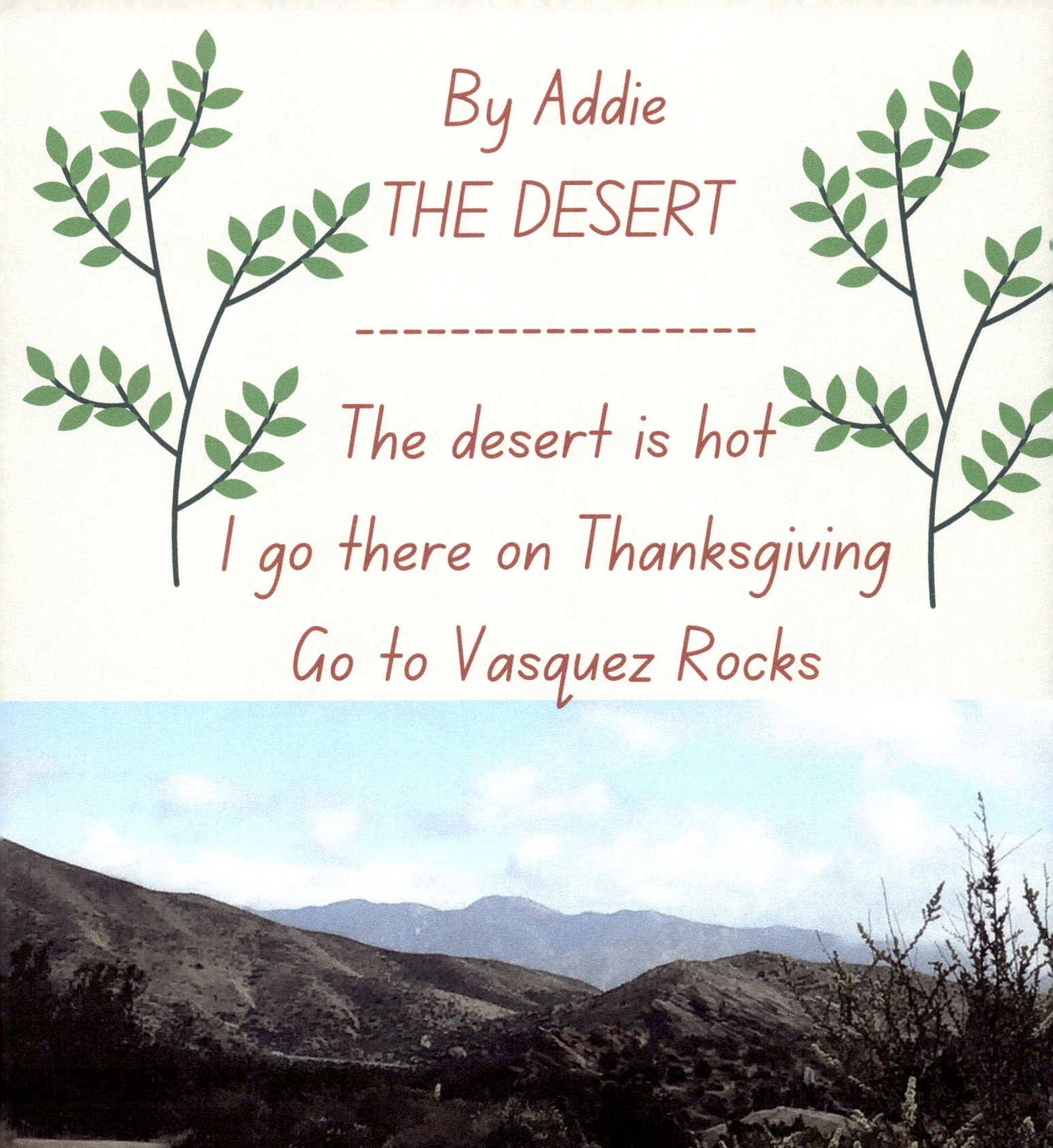

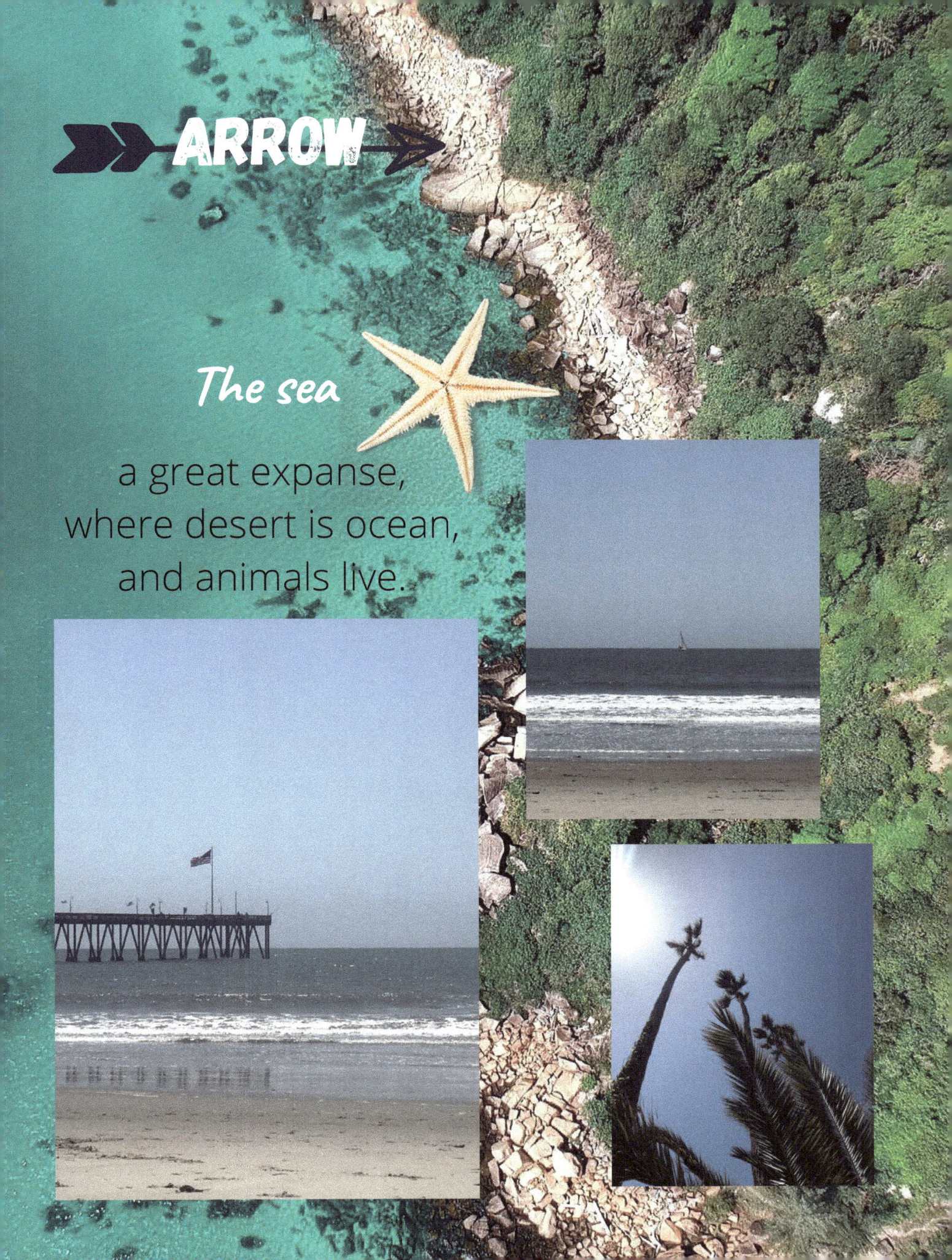

# ARROW

The sea

a great expanse,
where desert is ocean,
and animals live.

# BY AVERI

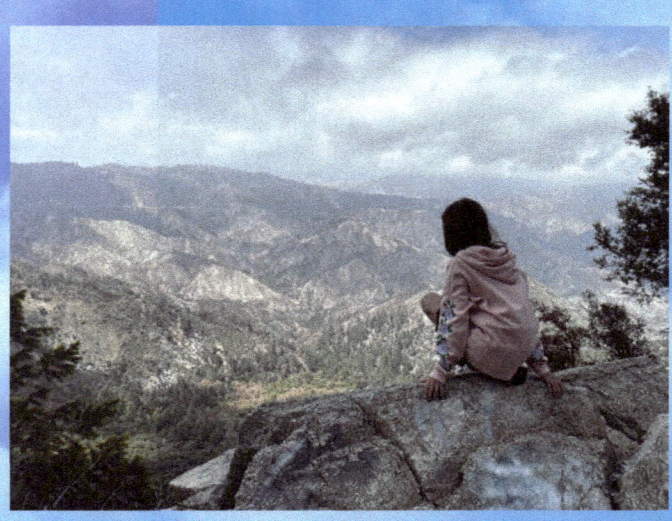

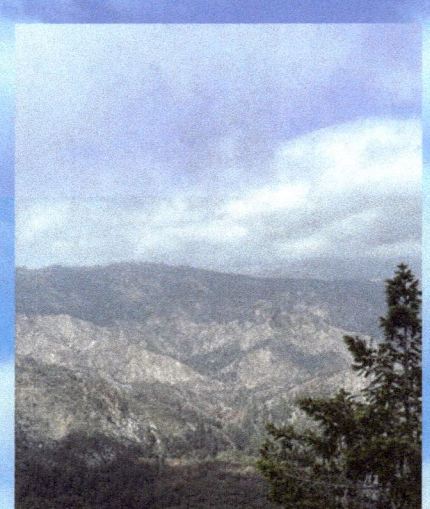

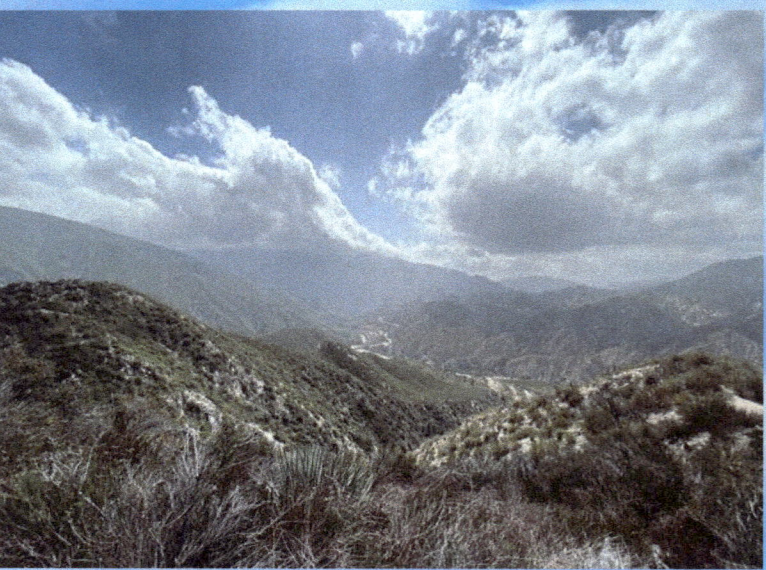

chaparral and clouds
tucked in between the mountains
wet mist fills the air

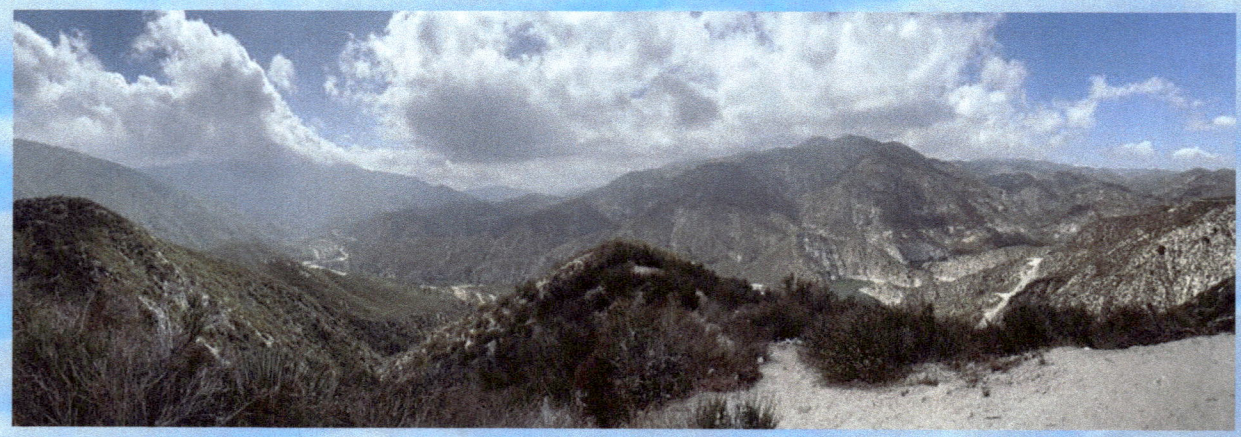

## By Bella

The Golden City is full of light, with many towers shining bright. Columbus Tower oh so pretty. Ferry Tower oh so nice in the middle of the night.

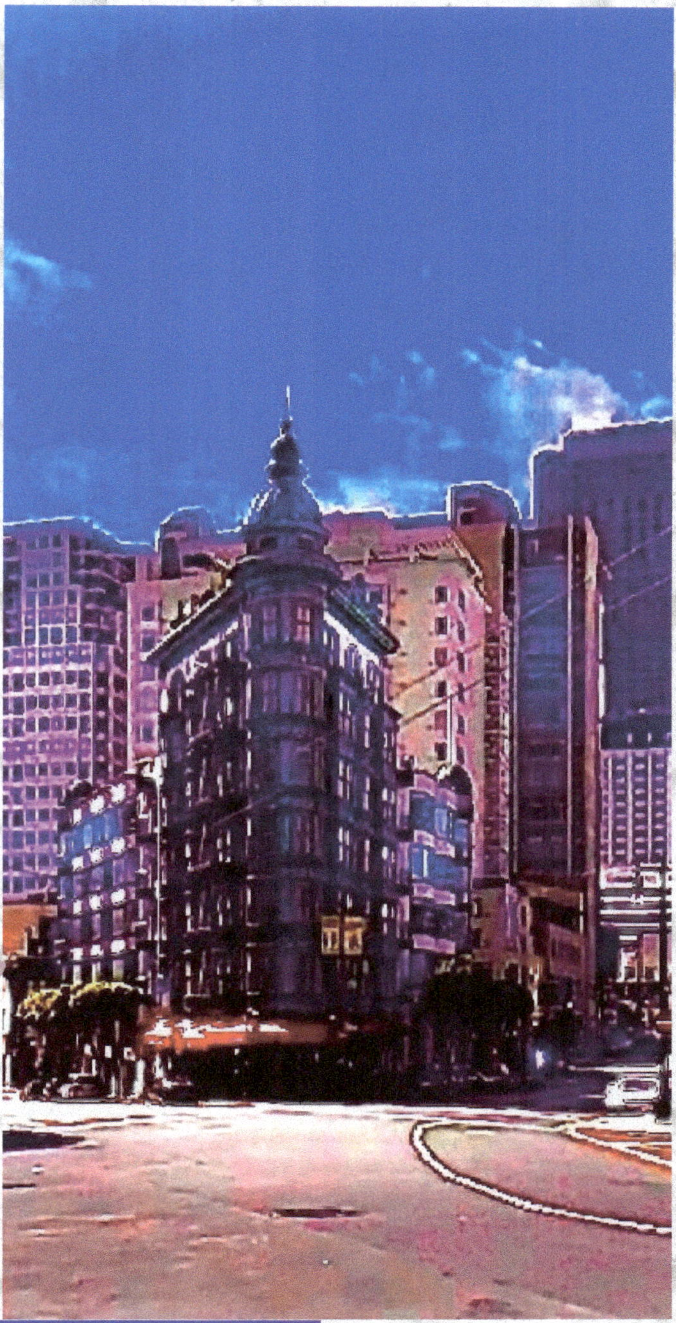

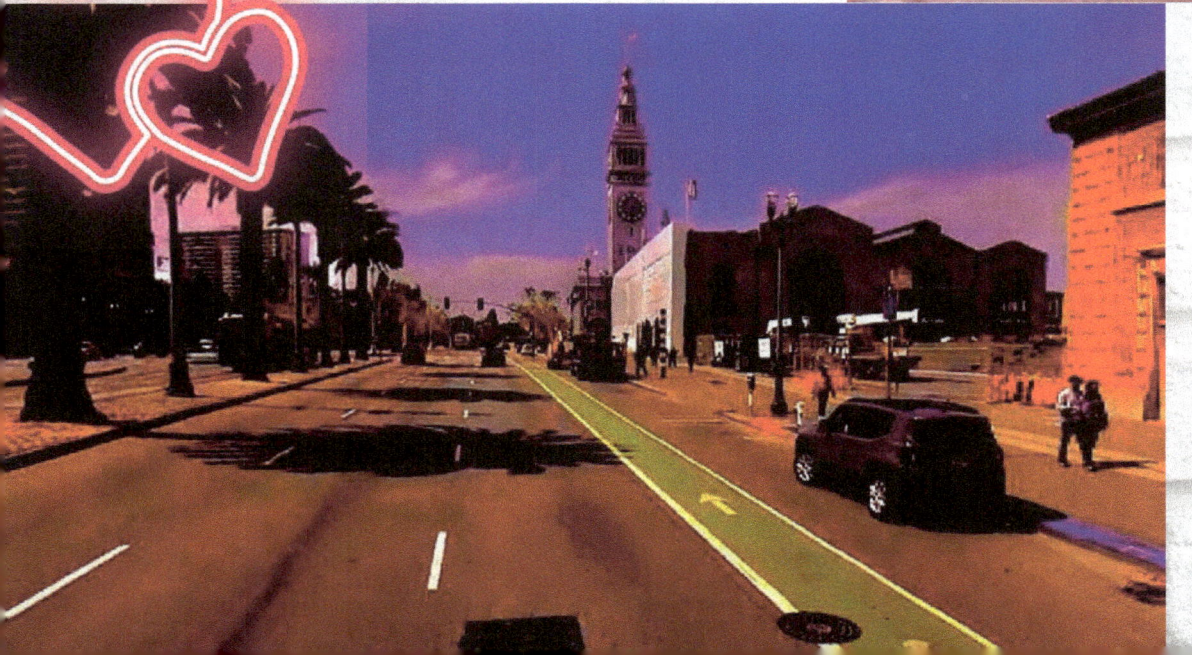

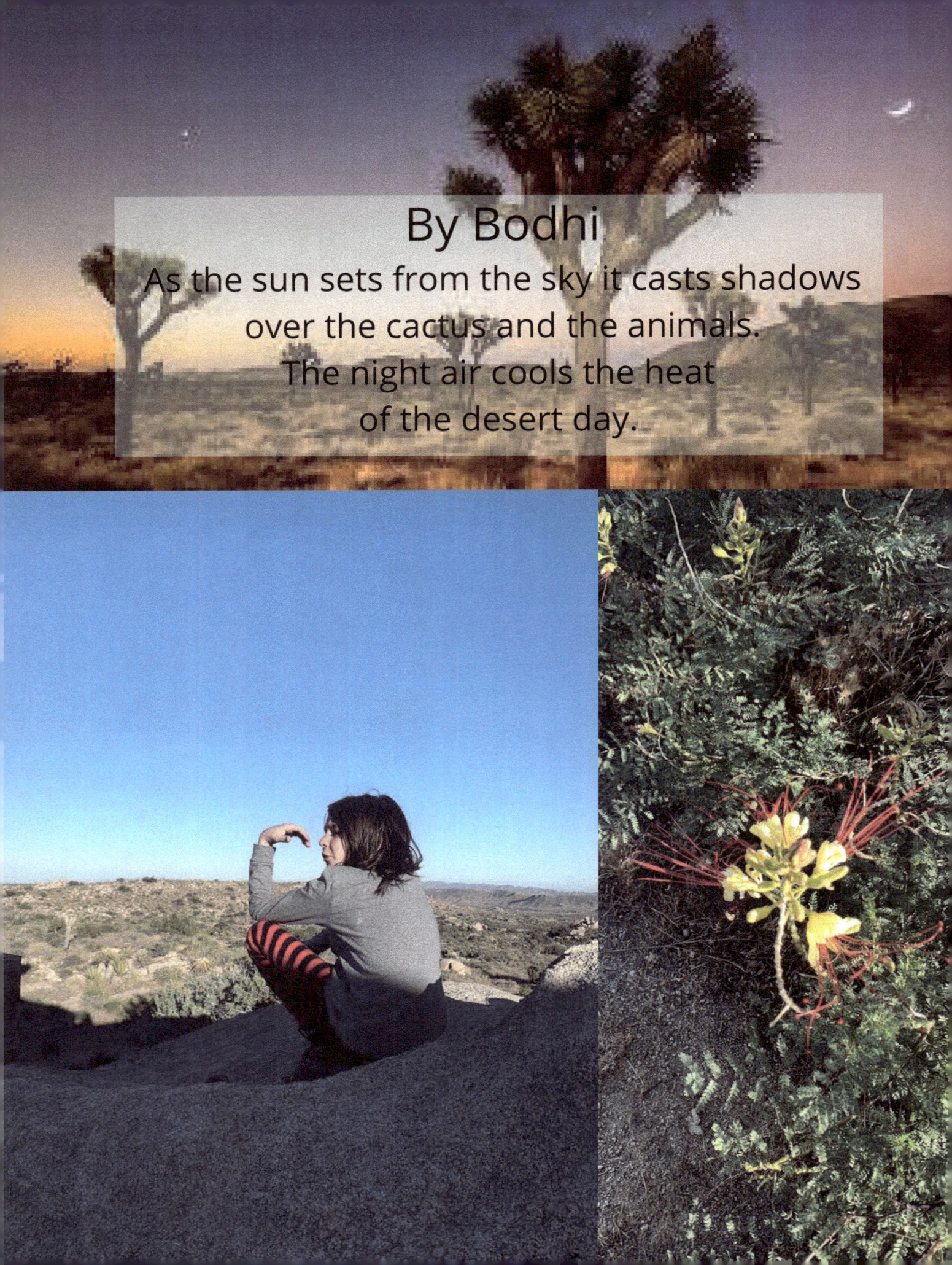

## By Bodhi

As the sun sets from the sky it casts shadows
over the cactus and the animals.
The night air cools the heat
of the desert day.

# By Camilo

When I got there I was running, playing, and walking. I first found a big tree so I hugged it so I can bring love to the tree.The second thing I did was to lie down in this big ravine. I walked carefully in the tree bridge. The third thing I did was to pick up a big stick. Last thing I did was sitting down on a bench in peace.
THE END

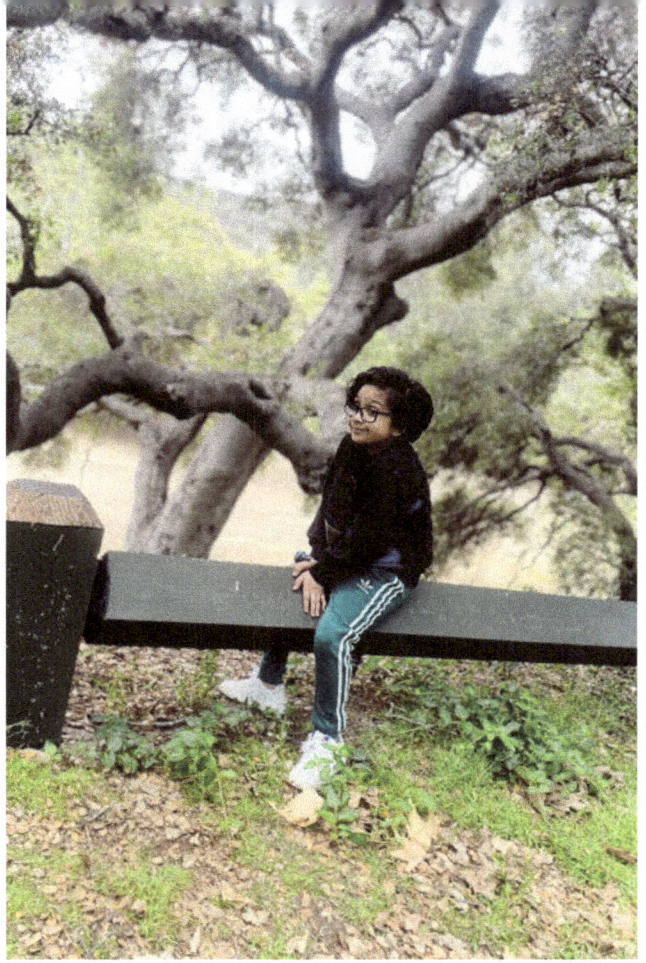

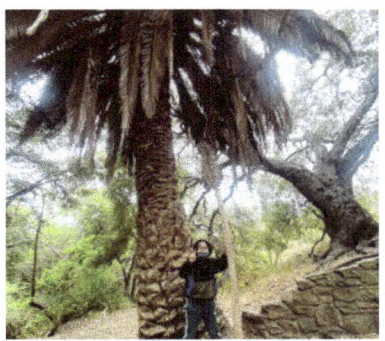

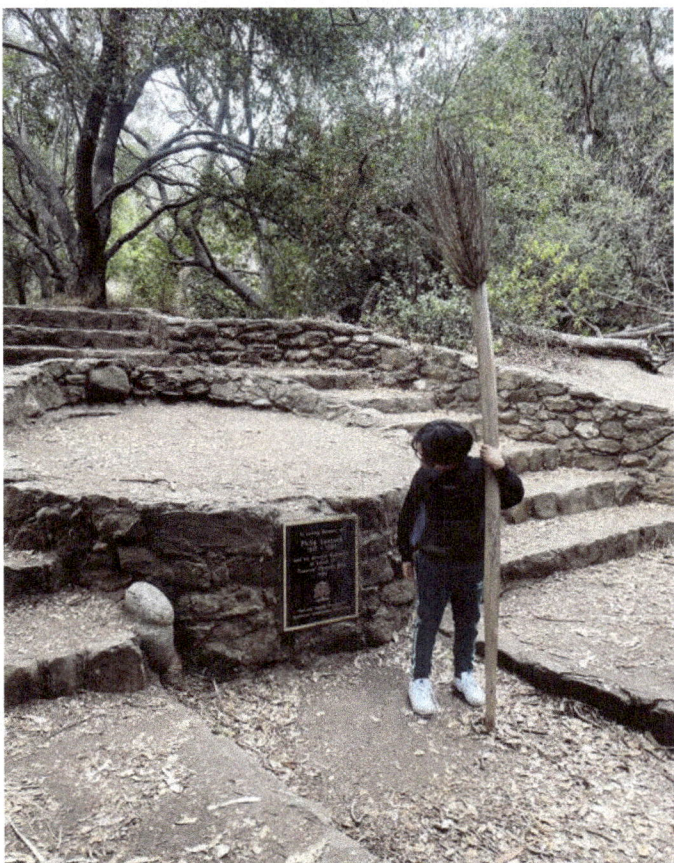

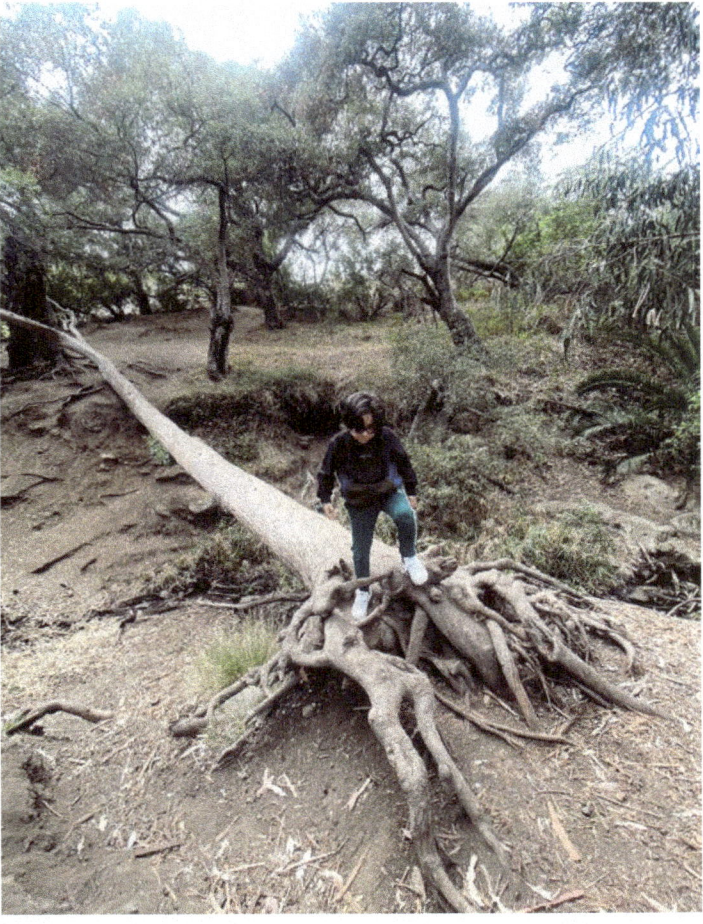

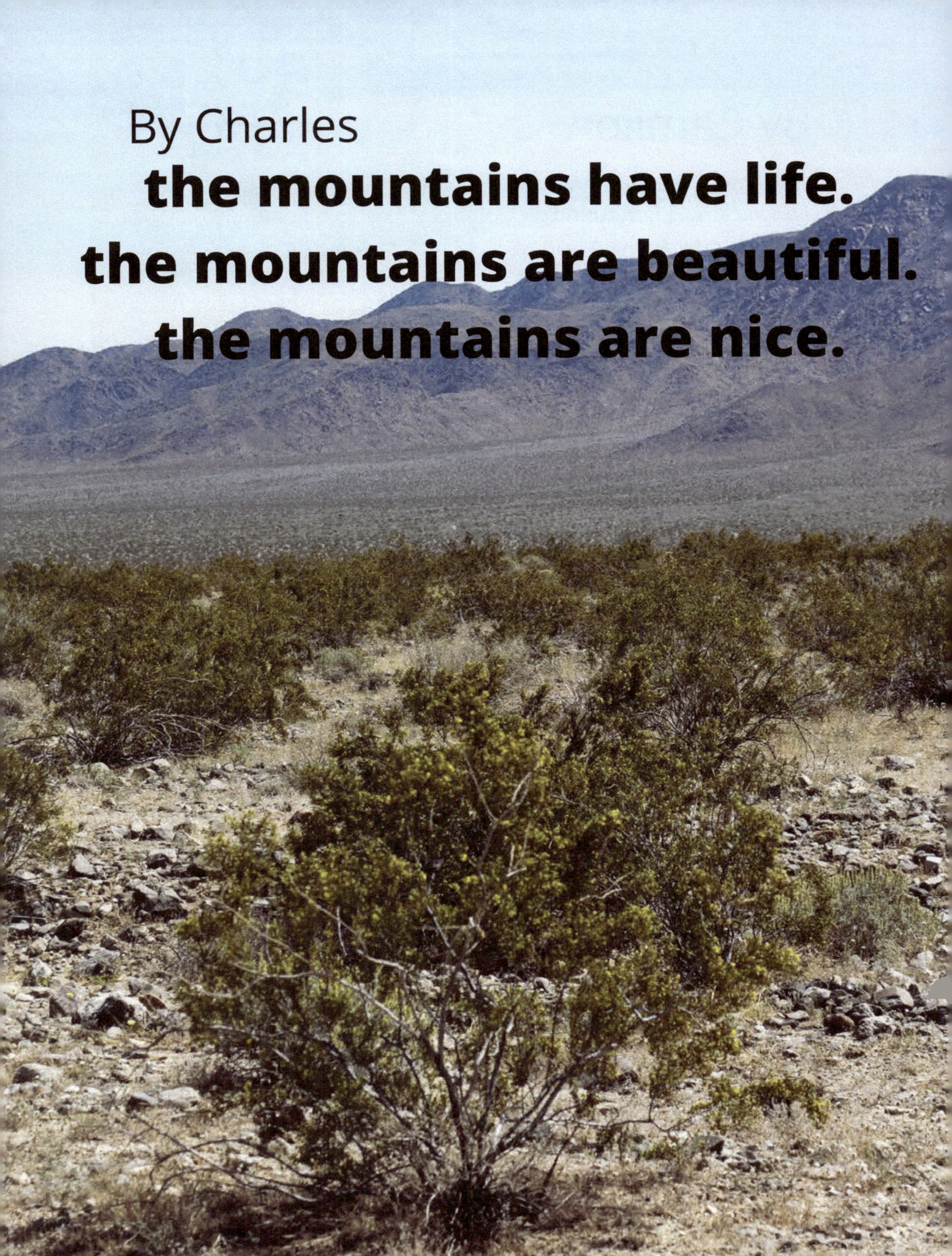

By Charles

**the mountains have life.**
**the mountains are beautiful.**
**the mountains are nice.**

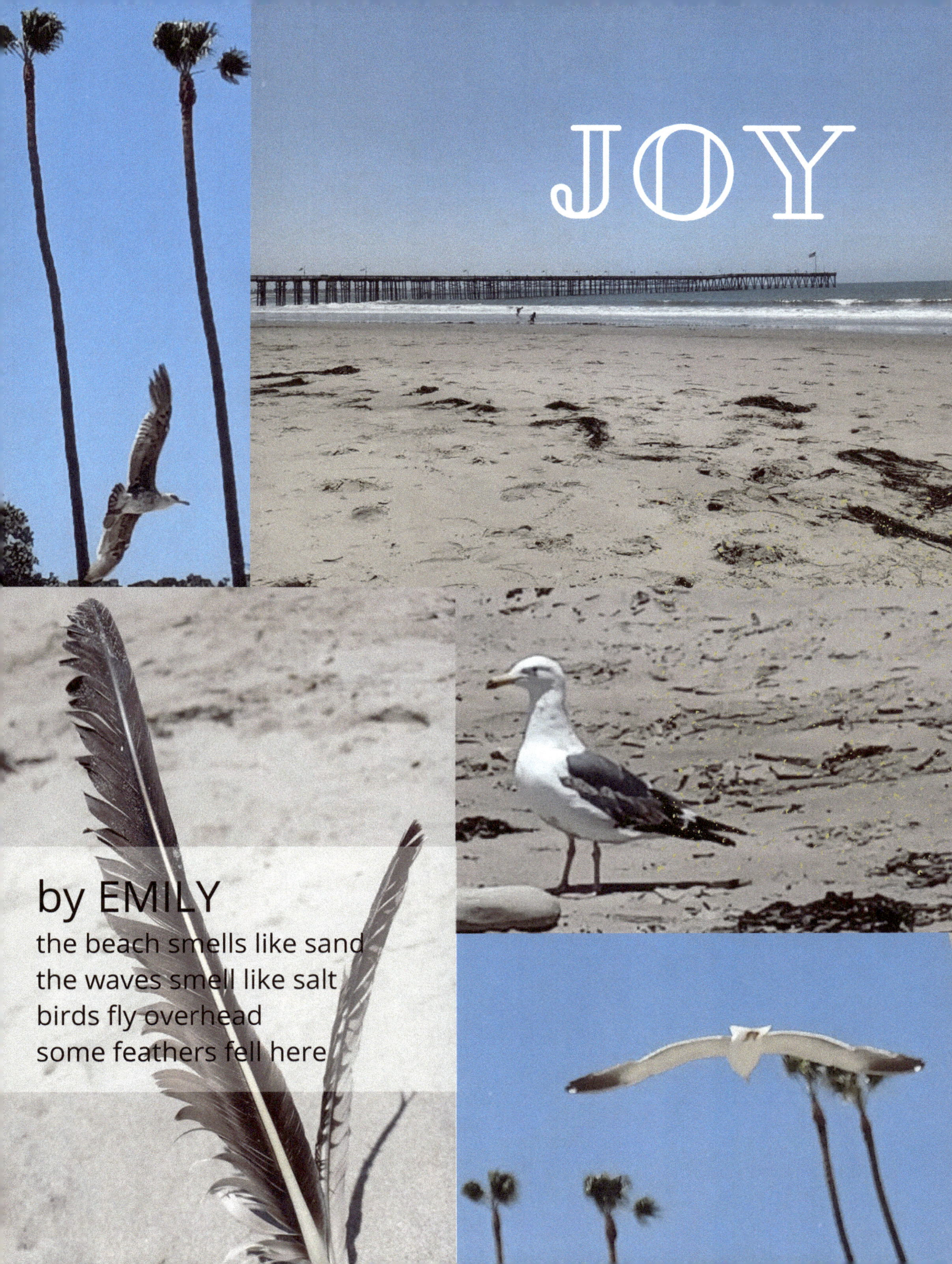

# JOY

## by EMILY

the beach smells like sand
the waves smell like salt
birds fly overhead
some feathers fell here

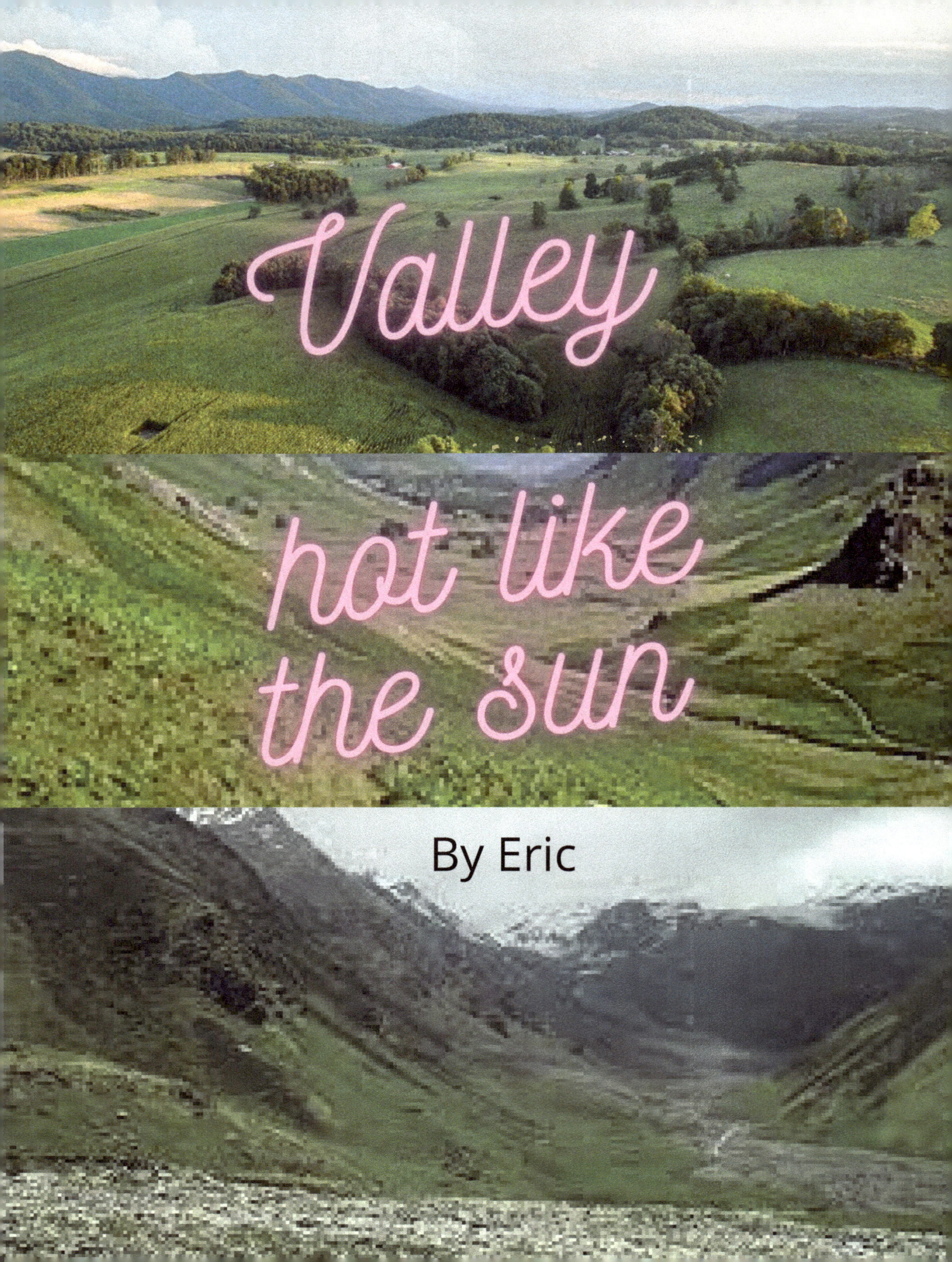

# Valley

## hot like the sun

By Eric

California
beaches

Sunset so
bright
California
beaches
what a
delight.

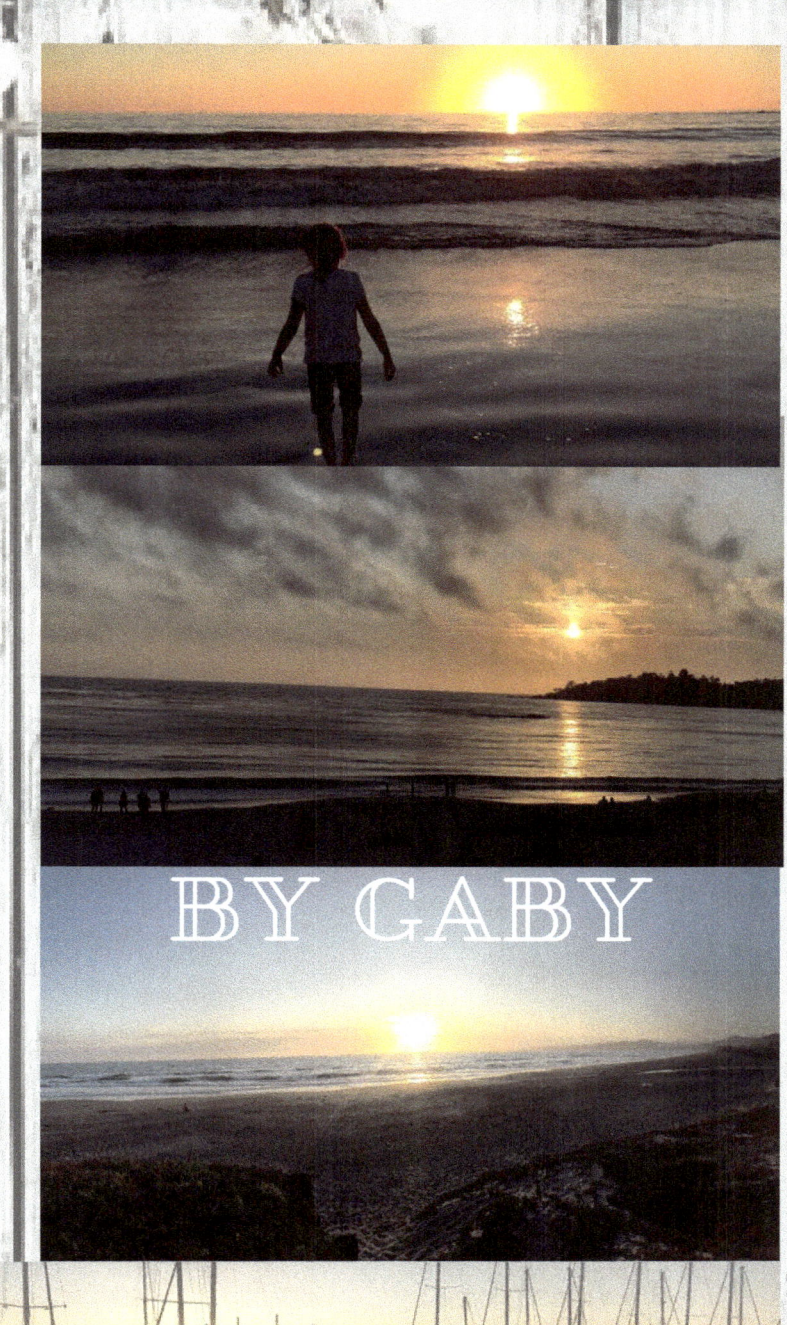

BY GABY

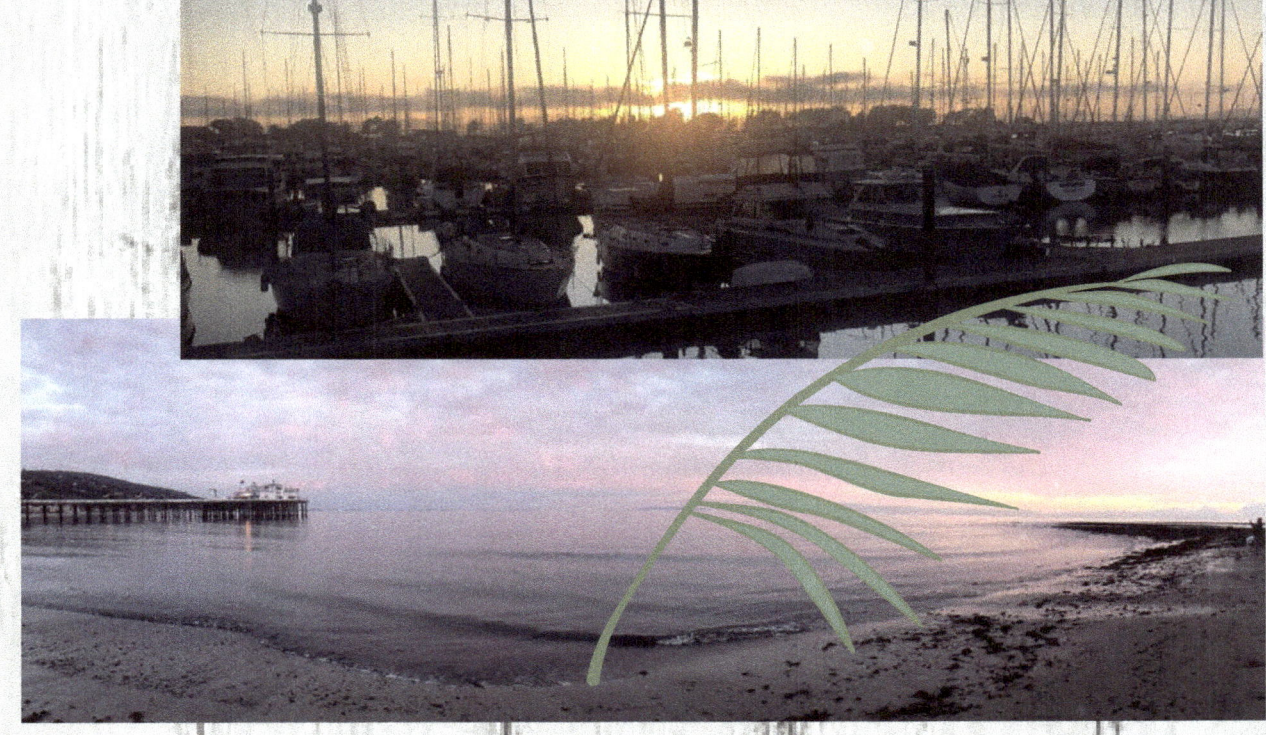

lovely mountains feel the air
breathe the air
feel the dirt and rocks
and be peaceful .

ISABELLA SANTIAGO

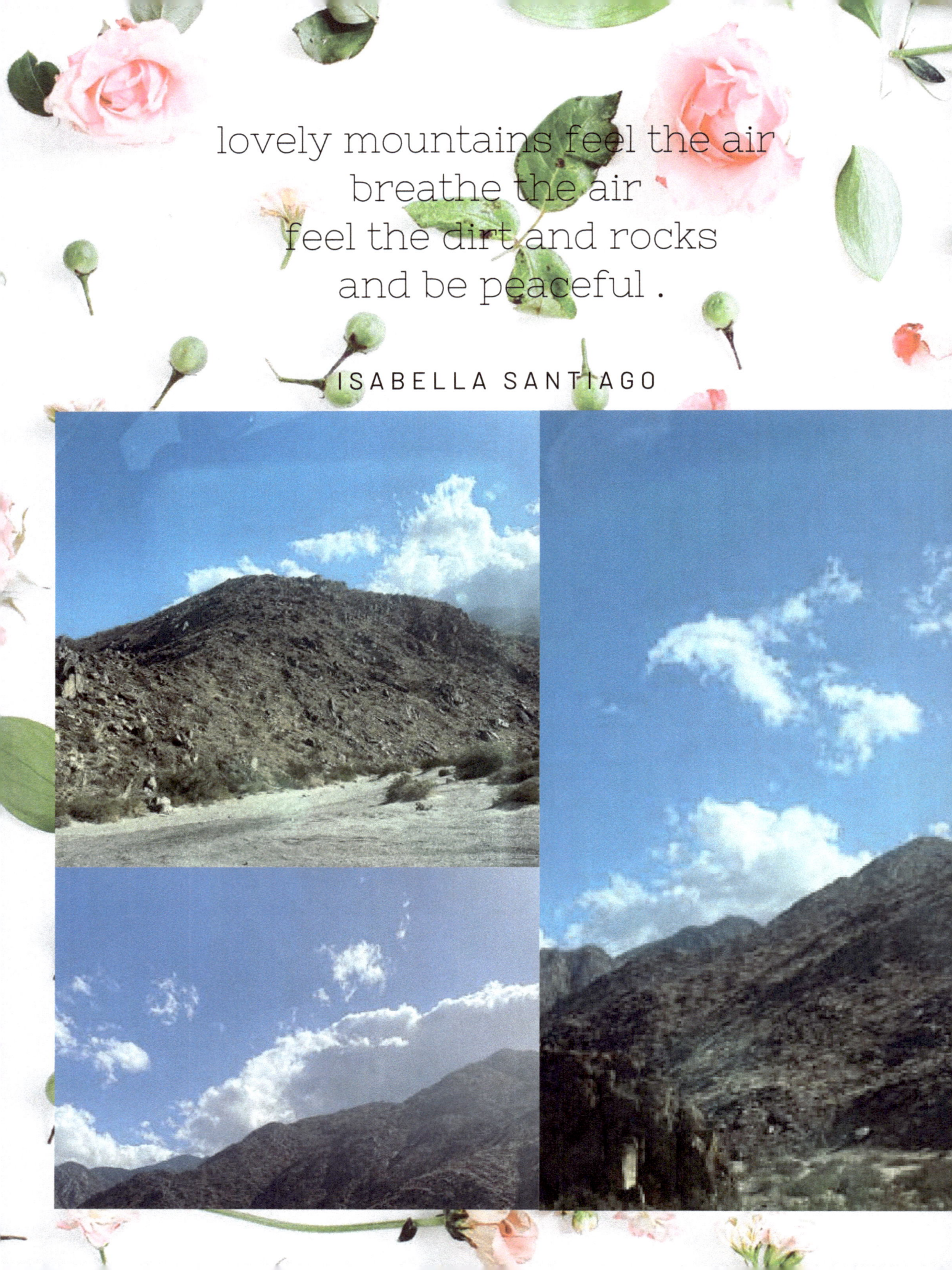

# Mountains

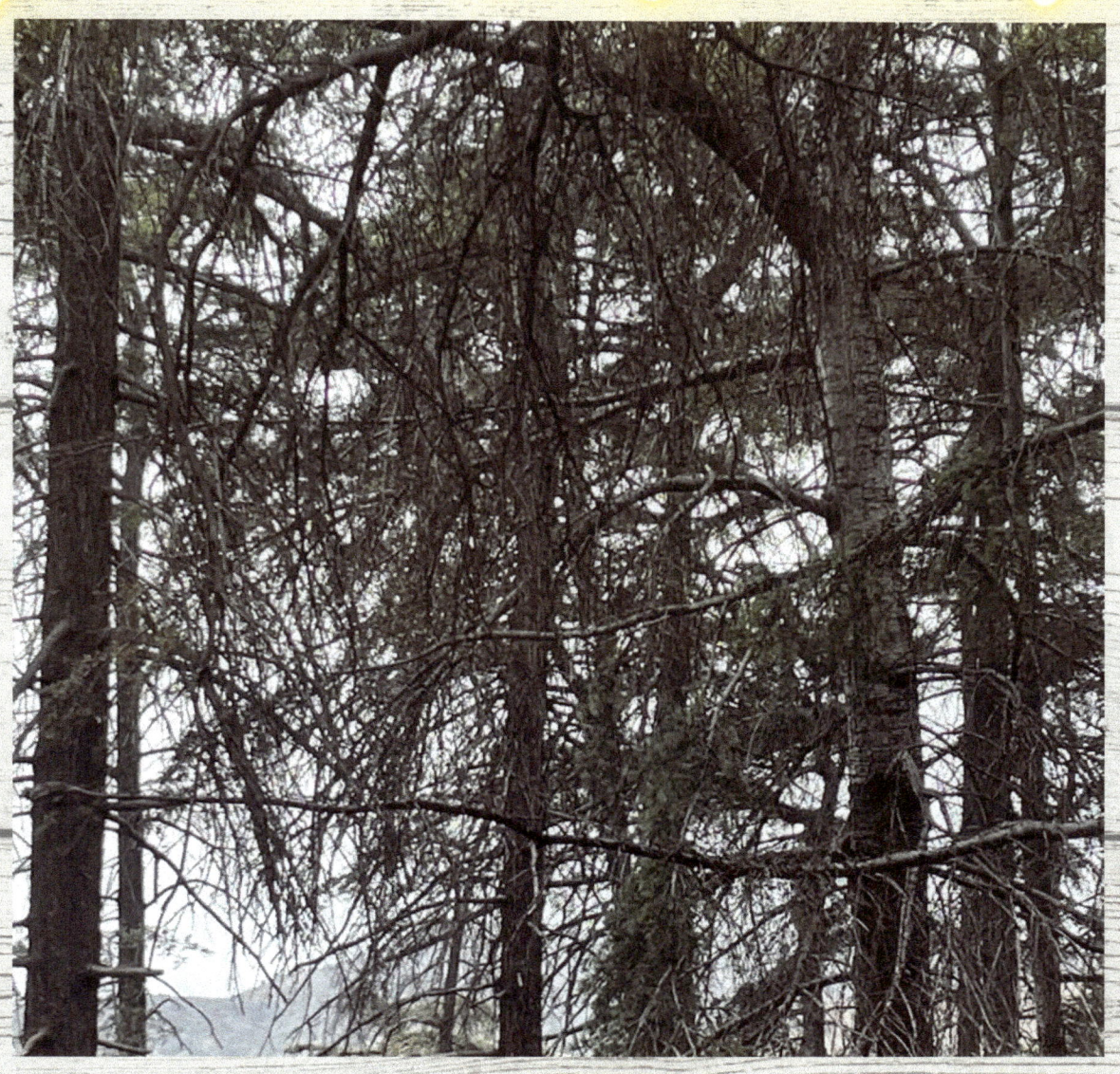

Beautiful mountain air,
with fresh smells of pine and wood.
A view of forest with trees
like skyscrapers
By June

By Leela

I'M ON THE BEACH

I'm on the beach, my legs are in the water, i feel
the breeze as i watch the beach calm down and get
sucked back to the ocean

# Luna

## The Lovely Coast

Lots and lots of cargo cranes

Super fun beaches

Lovely coast sunshine

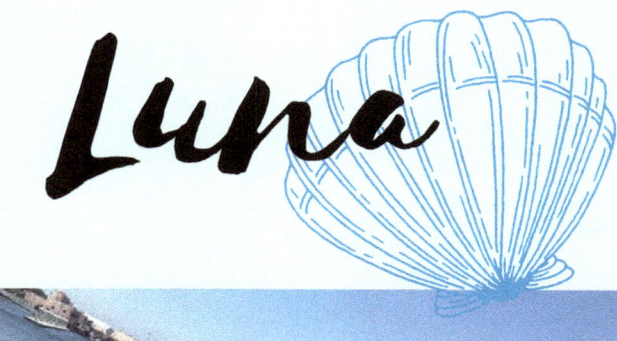

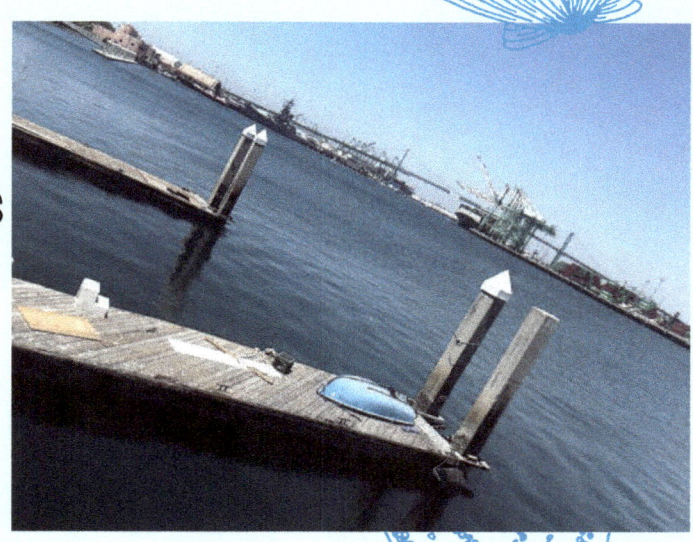

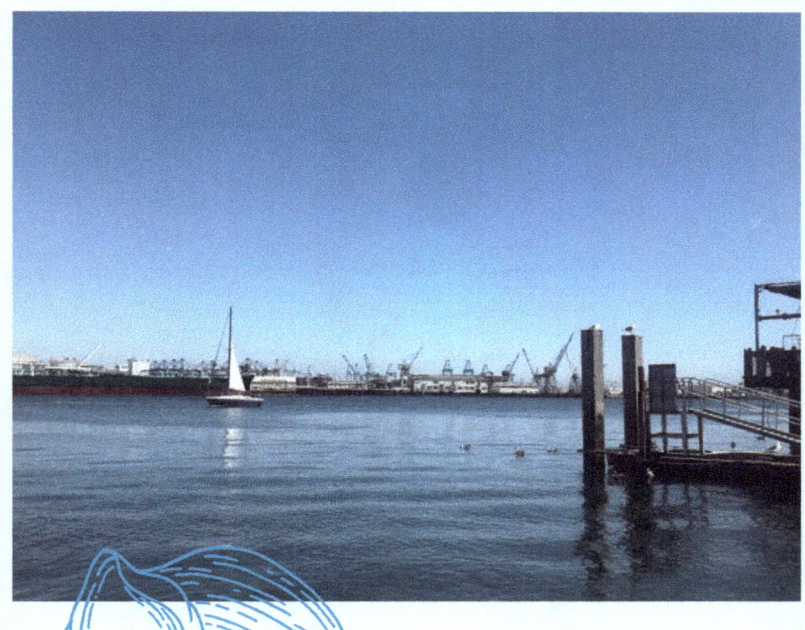

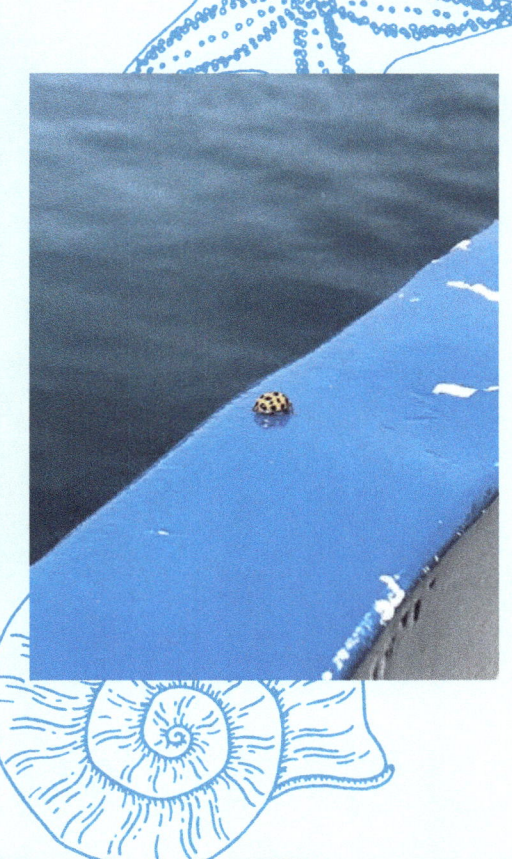

# By NYLA

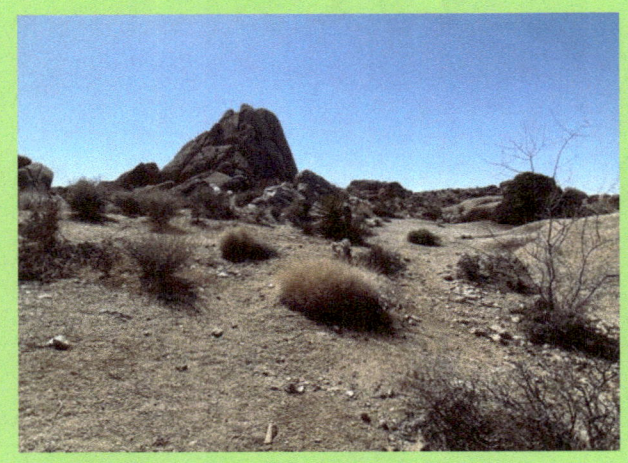

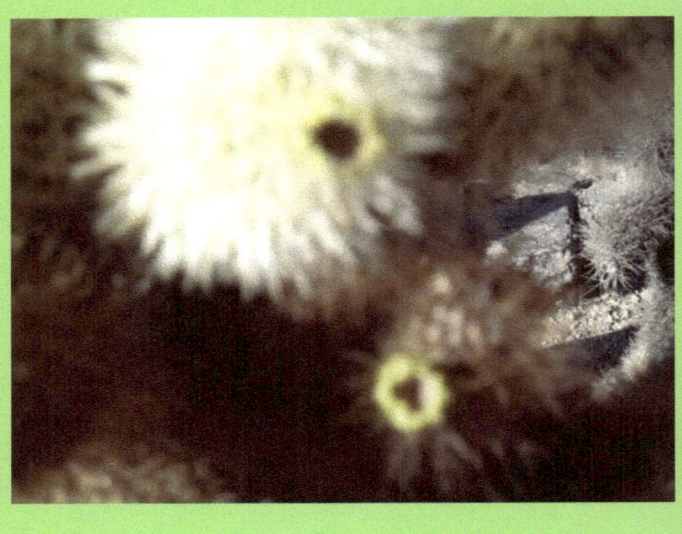

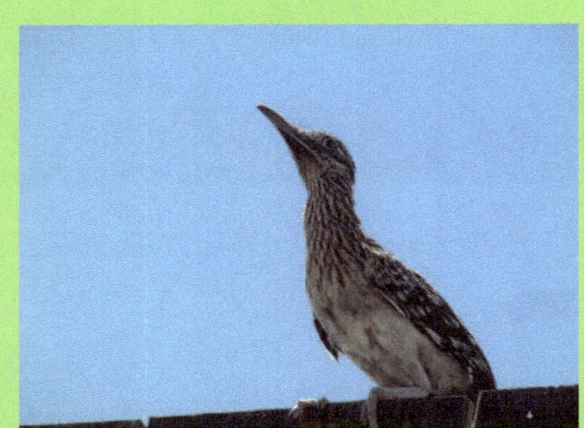

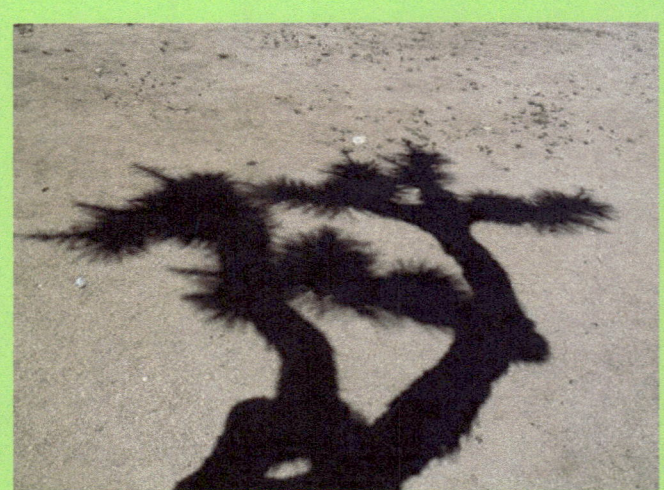

# Joshua tree

hot and humid air
animals running
everywhere
cactus spikes yikes

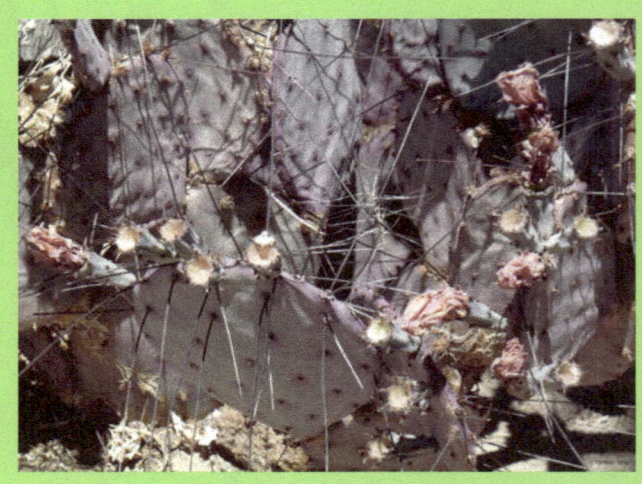

# BY TOWNES

## LITTLE LIZARD IN DISGUISE. CAN YOU SEE IT? SO CAN I.

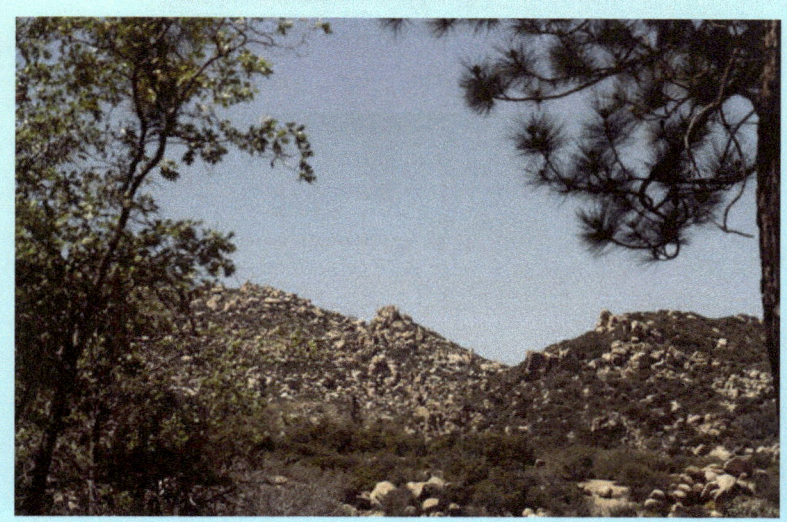

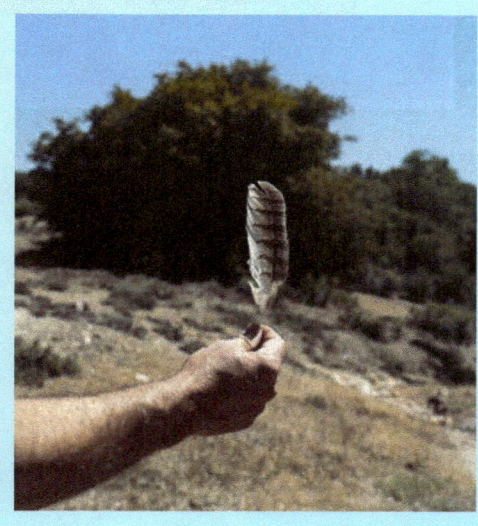

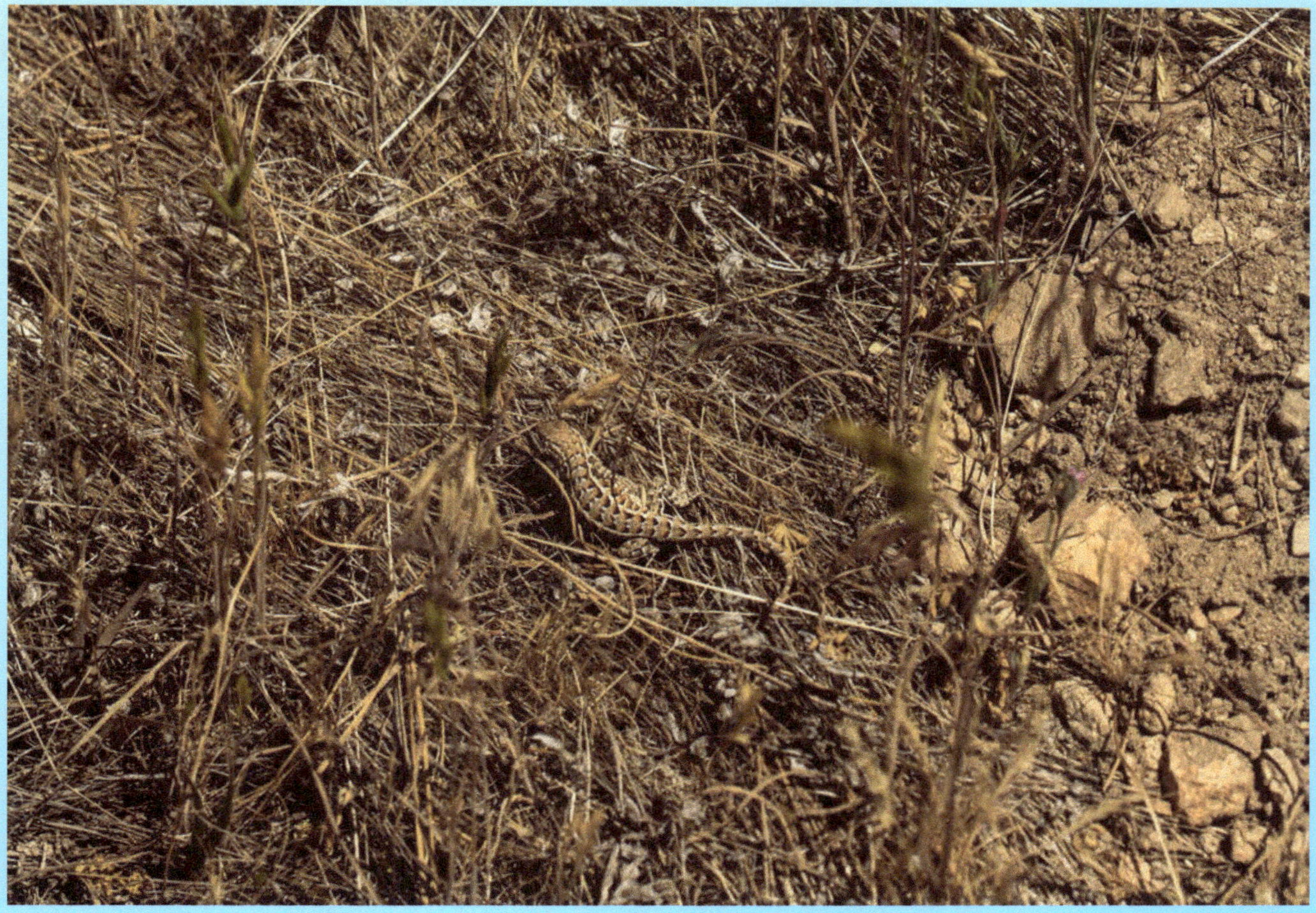

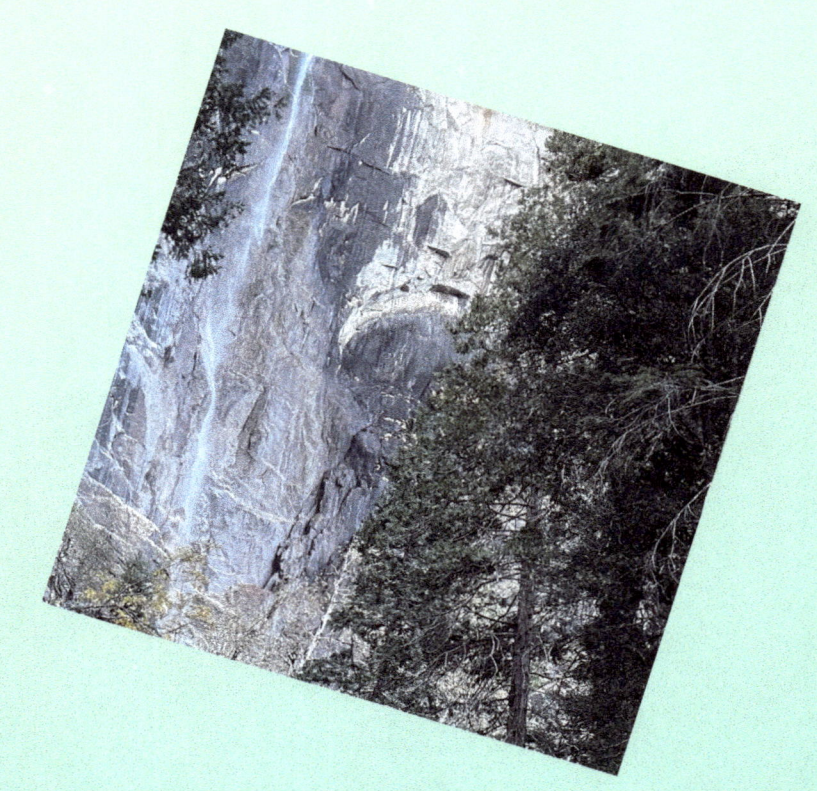

air blows my face and I
know I'm safe so let's
visit the mountains

BY SCARLETT

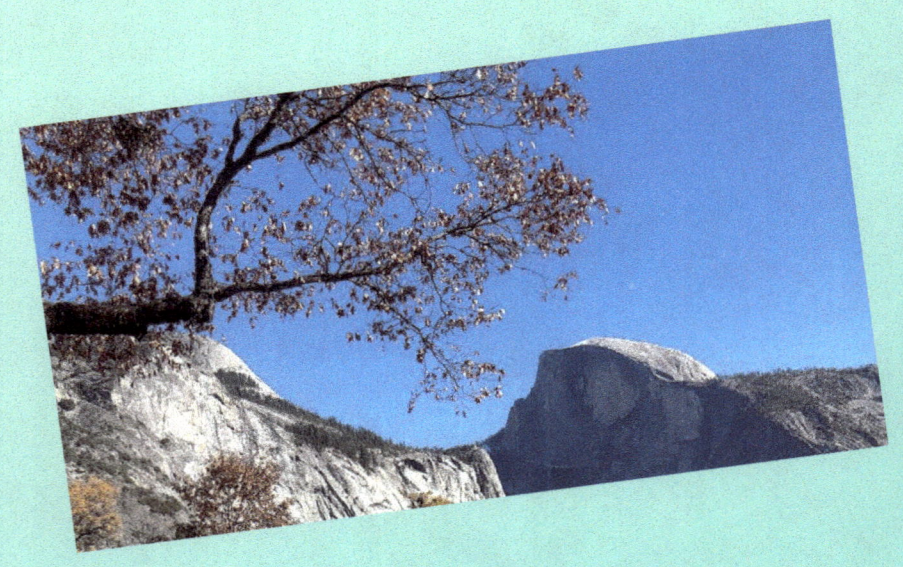

# By Valentino

**I feel the ocean on my feet
I  like to feel the cool cool breeze
If you go to the ocean, here I lie
to watch the sunset in the sky**

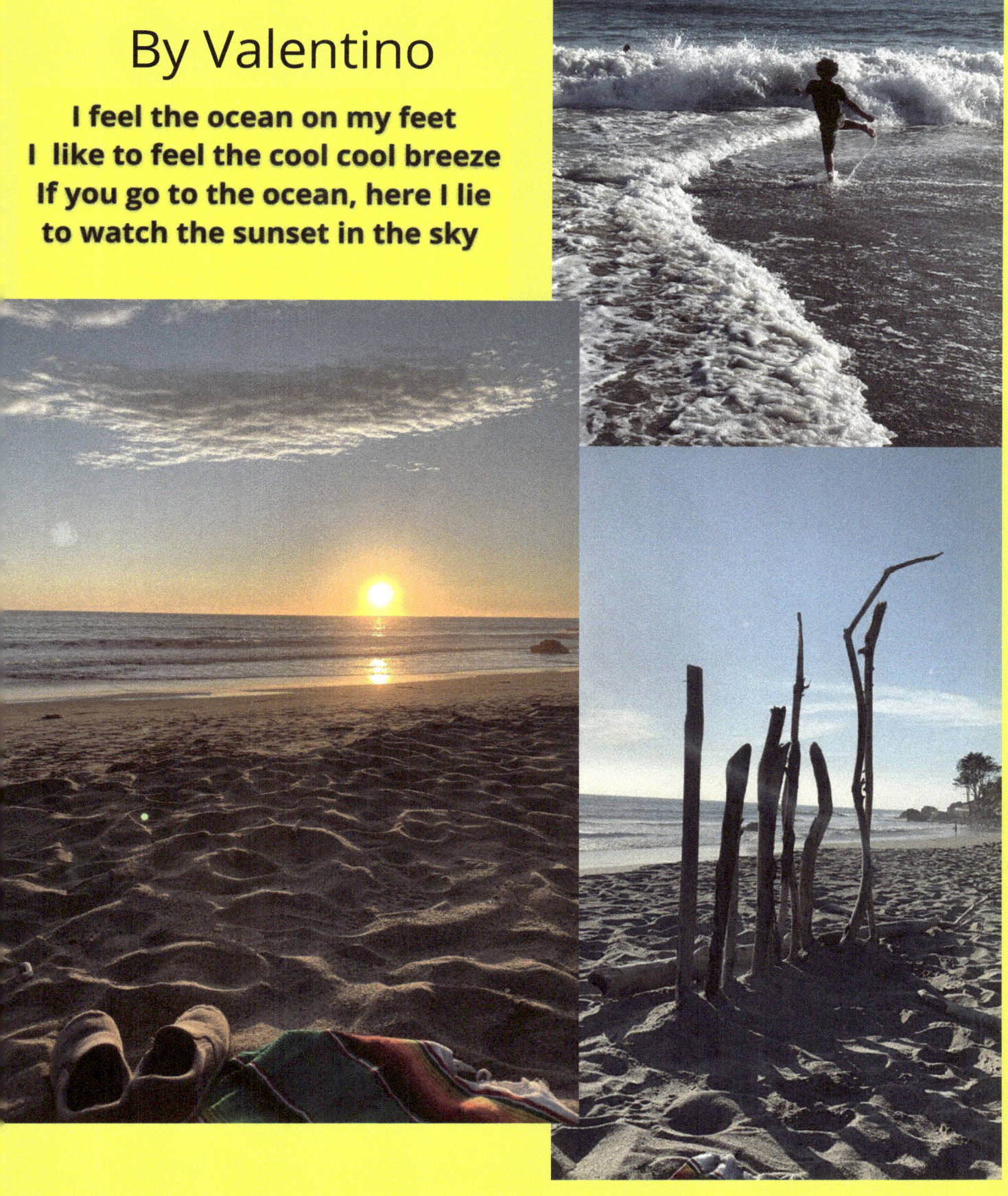

# the coast

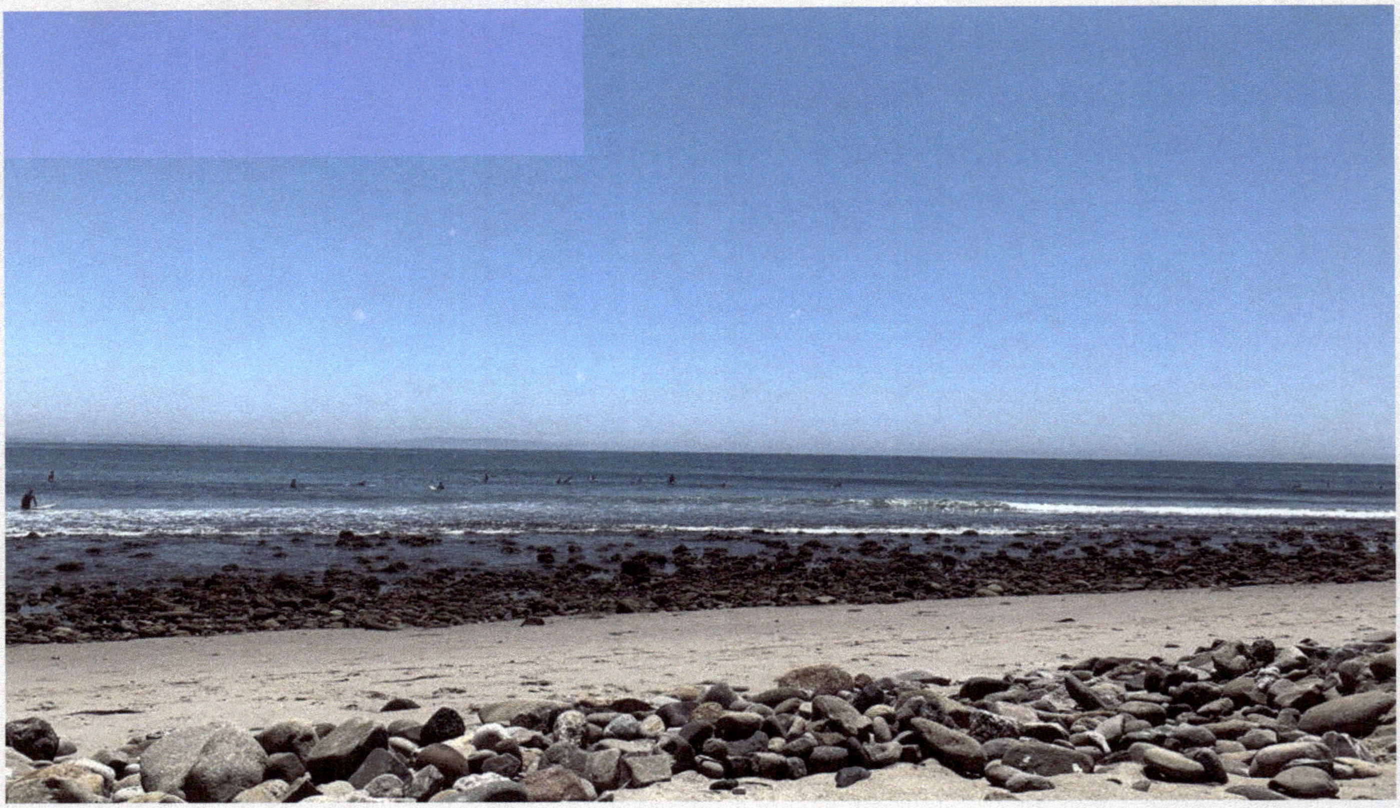

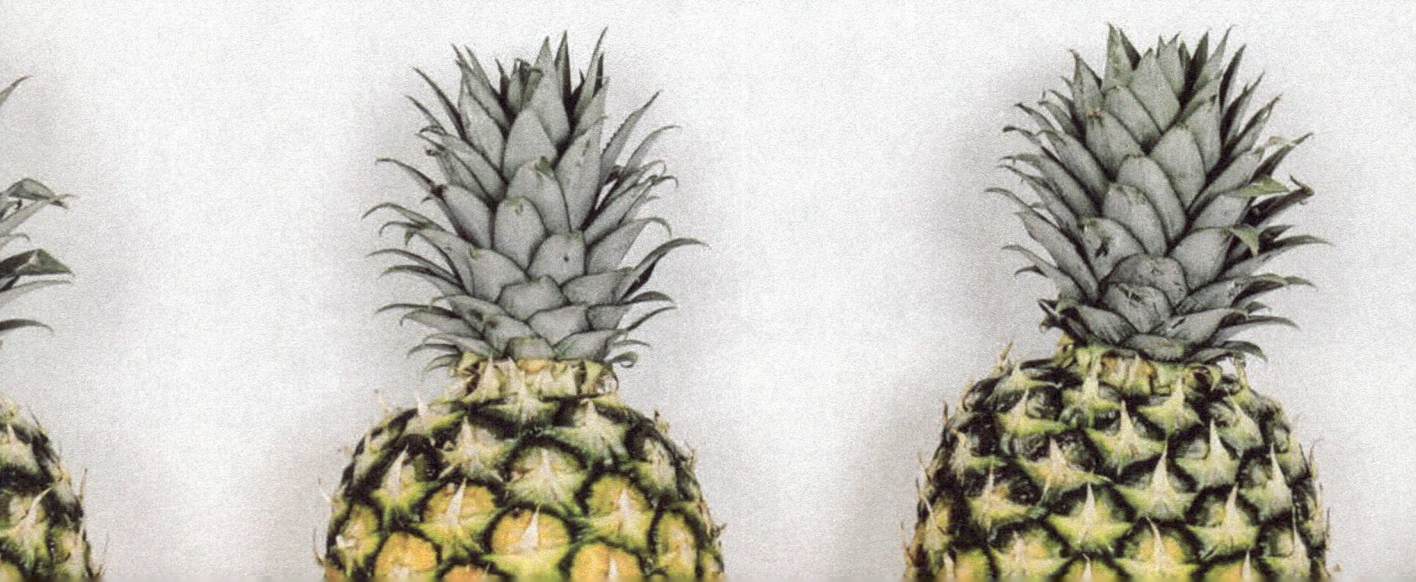

I don't like going to the coast in the night for in the dark I have a fright I like going in the day because I'm always ready to play.

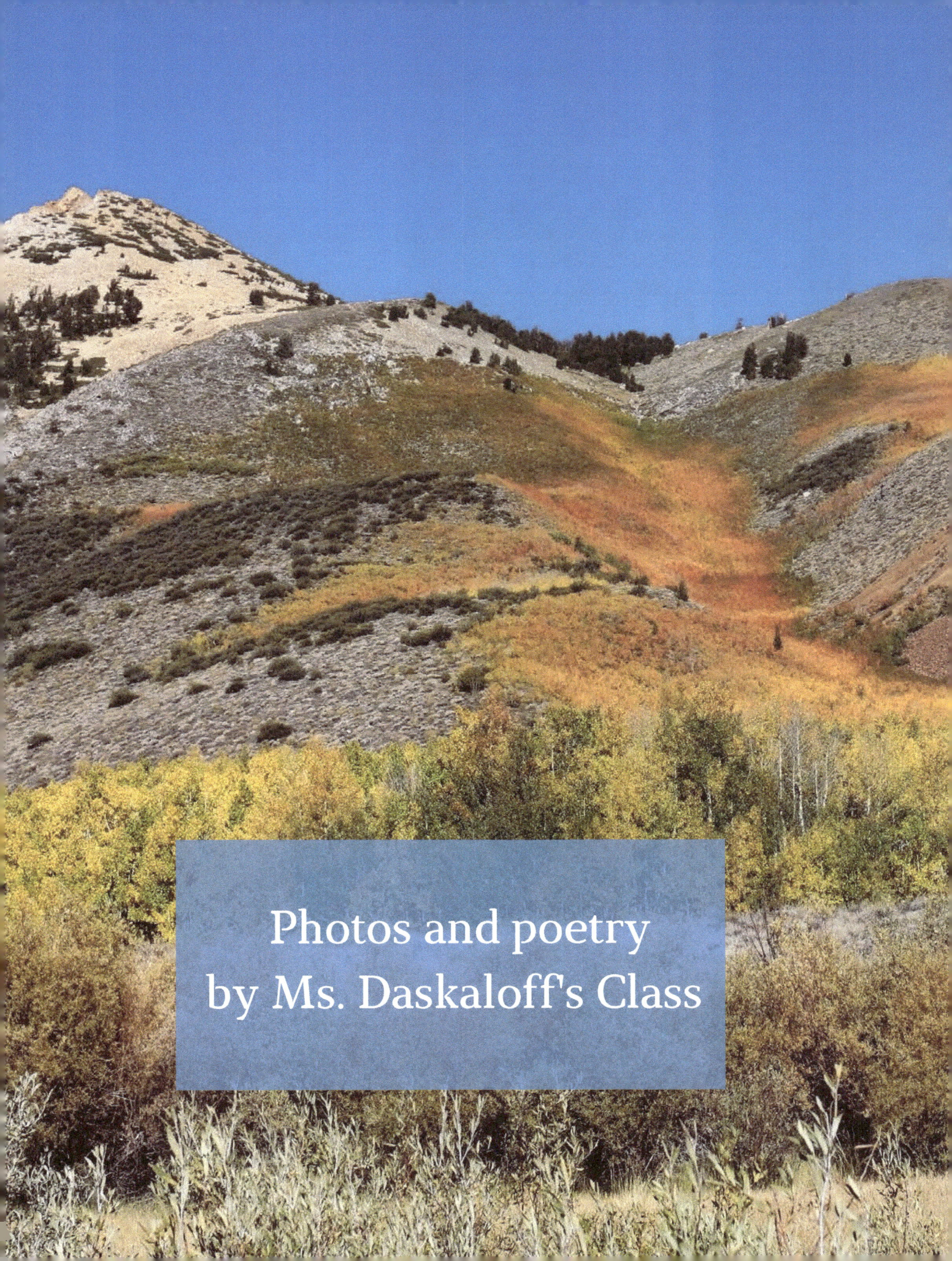

Photos and poetry
by Ms. Daskaloff's Class

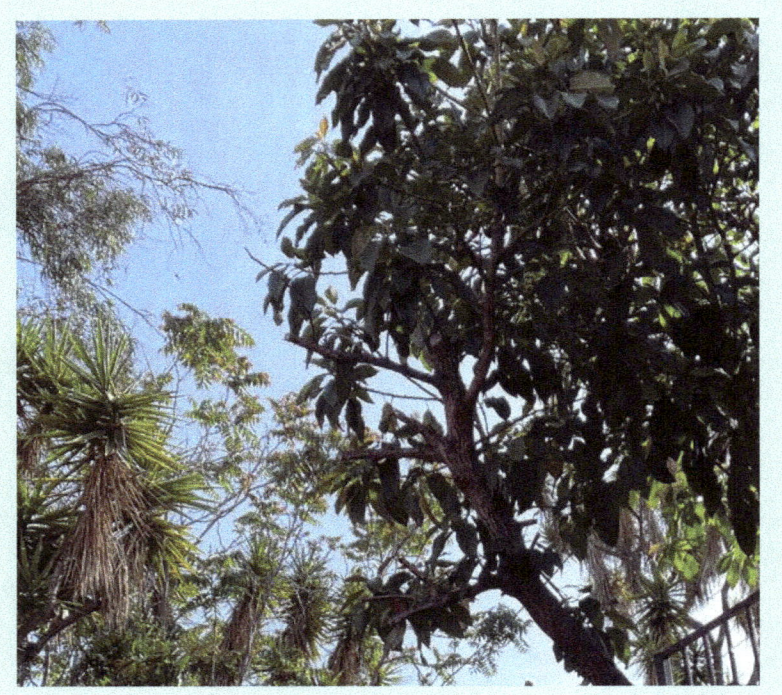

I am Aaliyah
I like flowers and roses
I also like trees

By Aaliyah

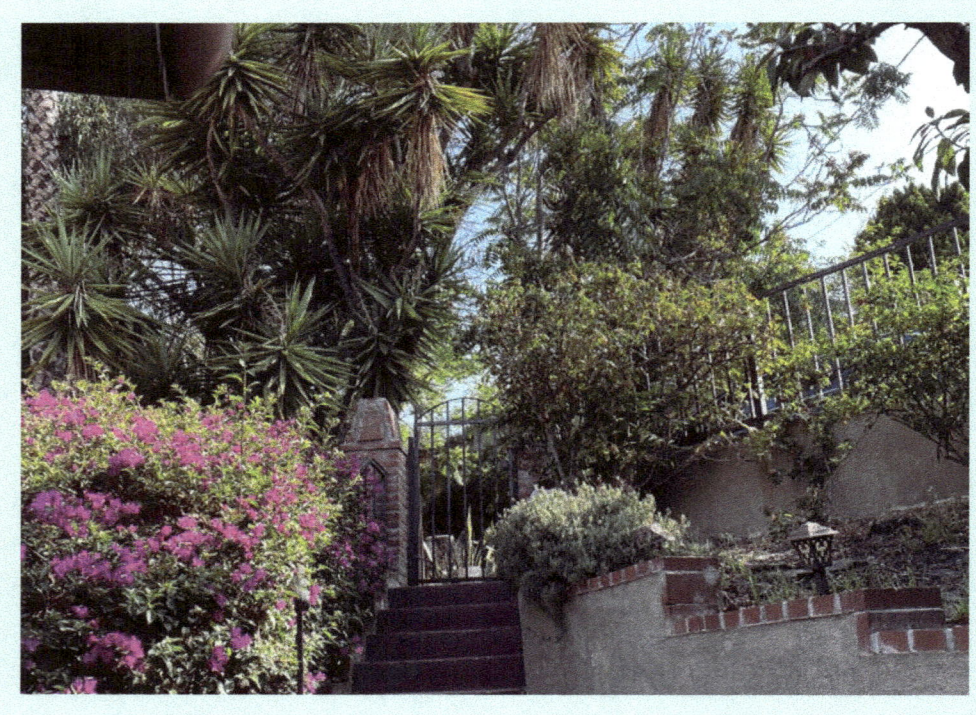

By Asher

# Oh Valley

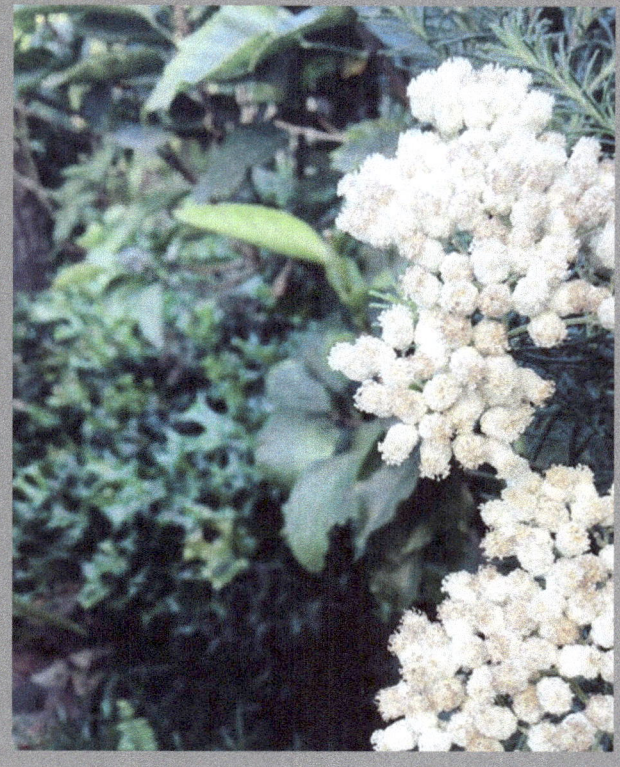

Valley oh valley
you are my home
you feed me
your crops oh
valley

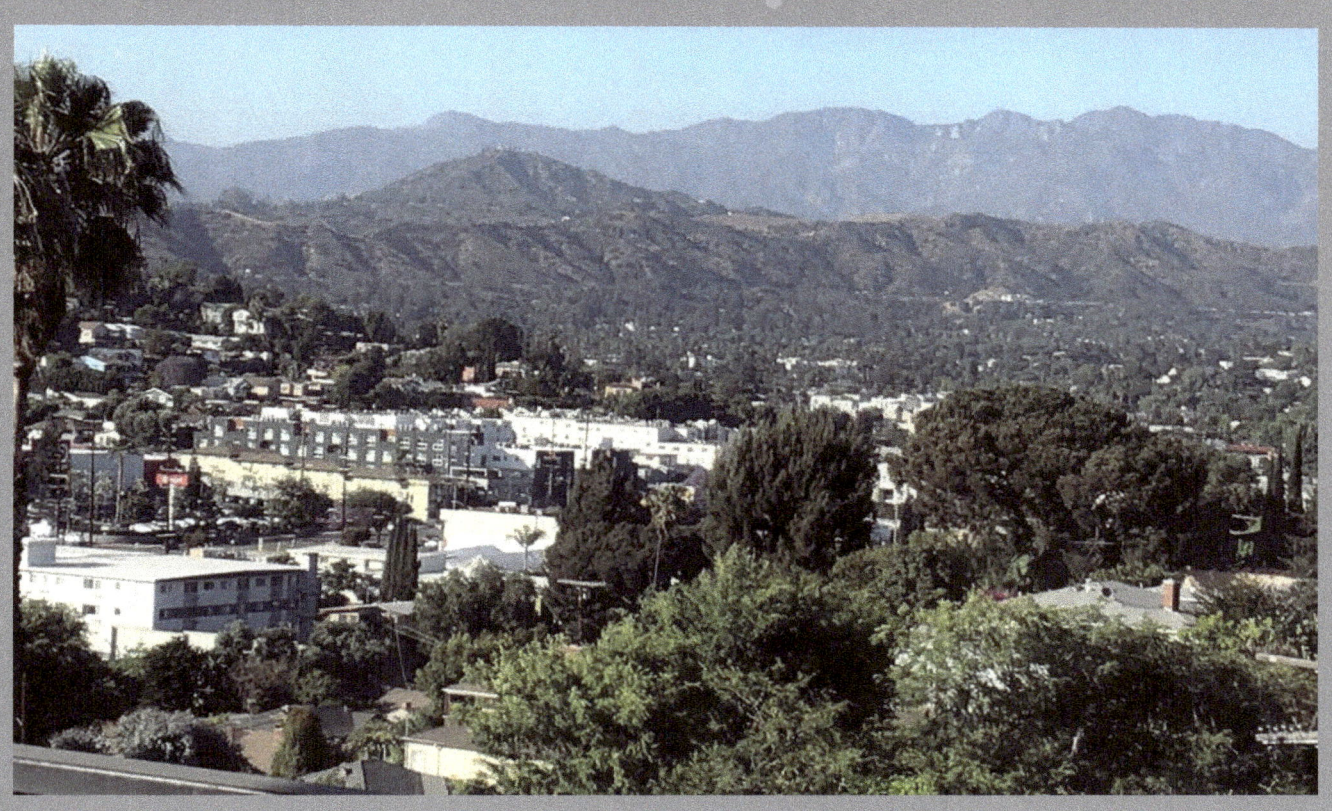

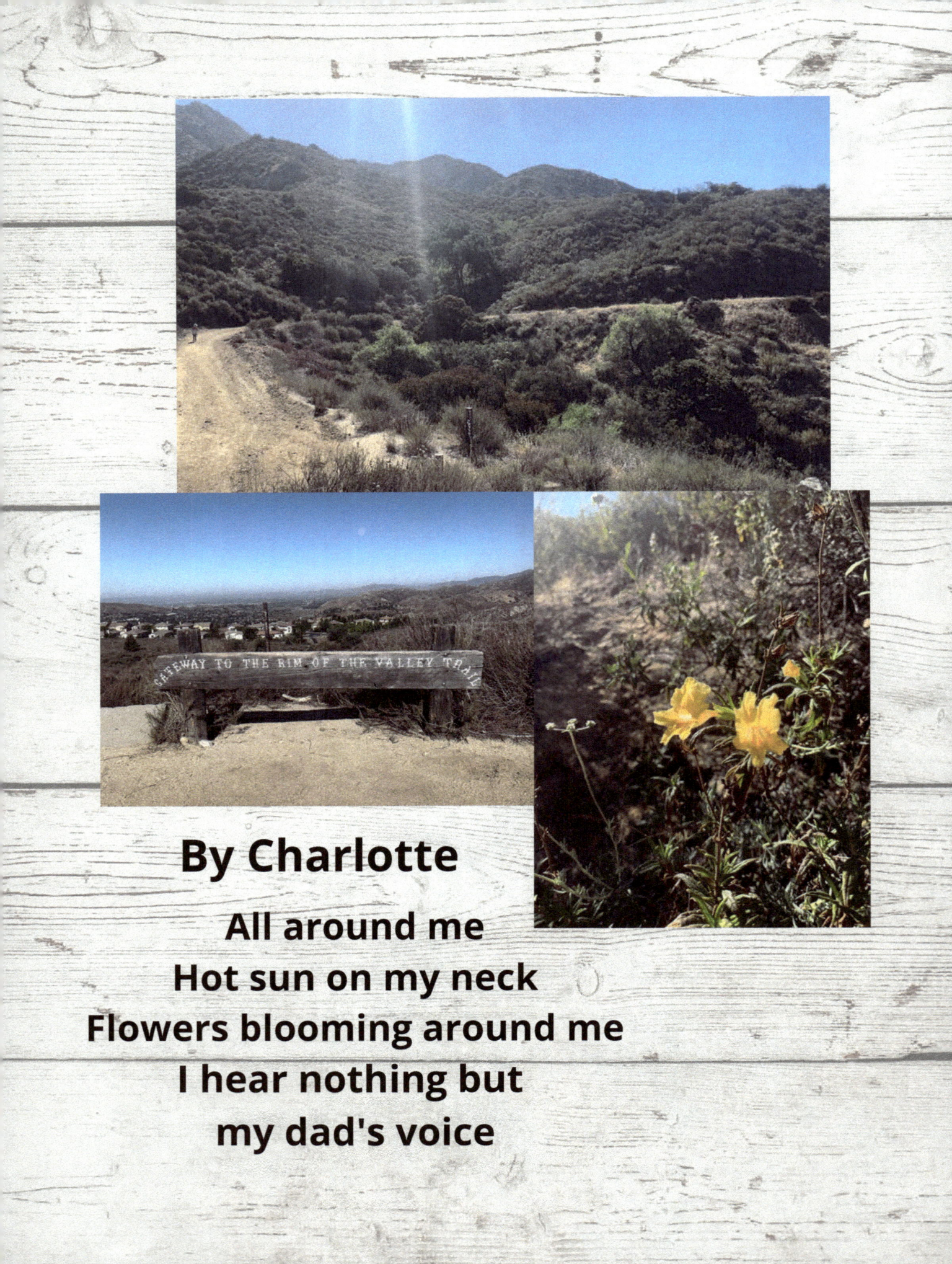

**By Charlotte**

All around me
Hot sun on my neck
Flowers blooming around me
I hear nothing but
my dad's voice

# DELILAH SANTIAGO

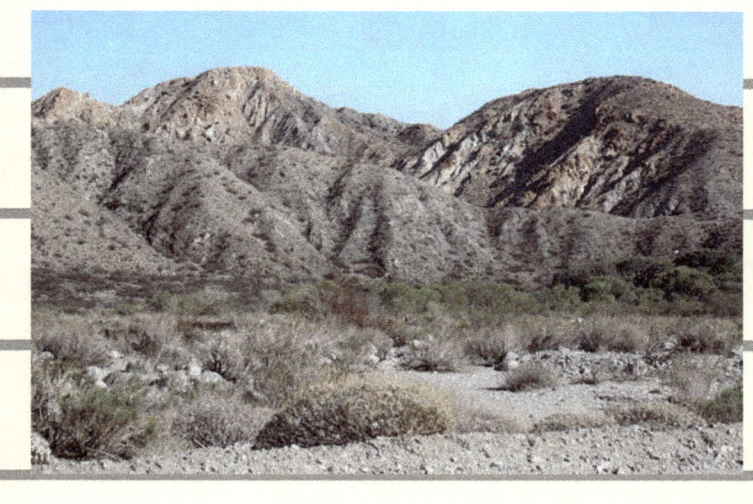

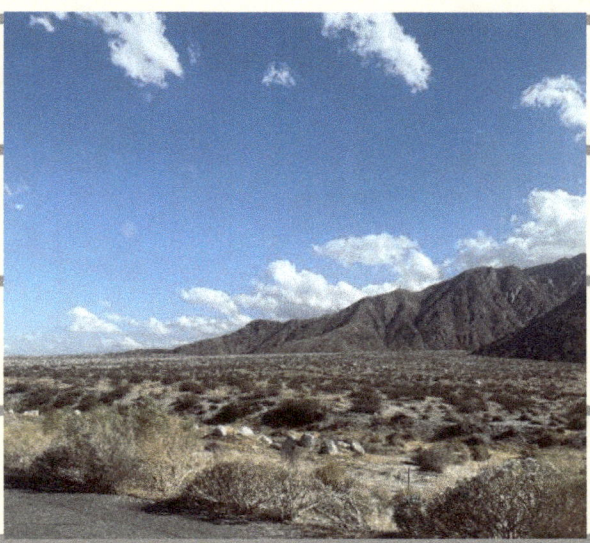

## SAND AND MOUNTAINS
## WHAT DO I SEE?
## A BIG YELLOW SUN
## SHINING AT ME

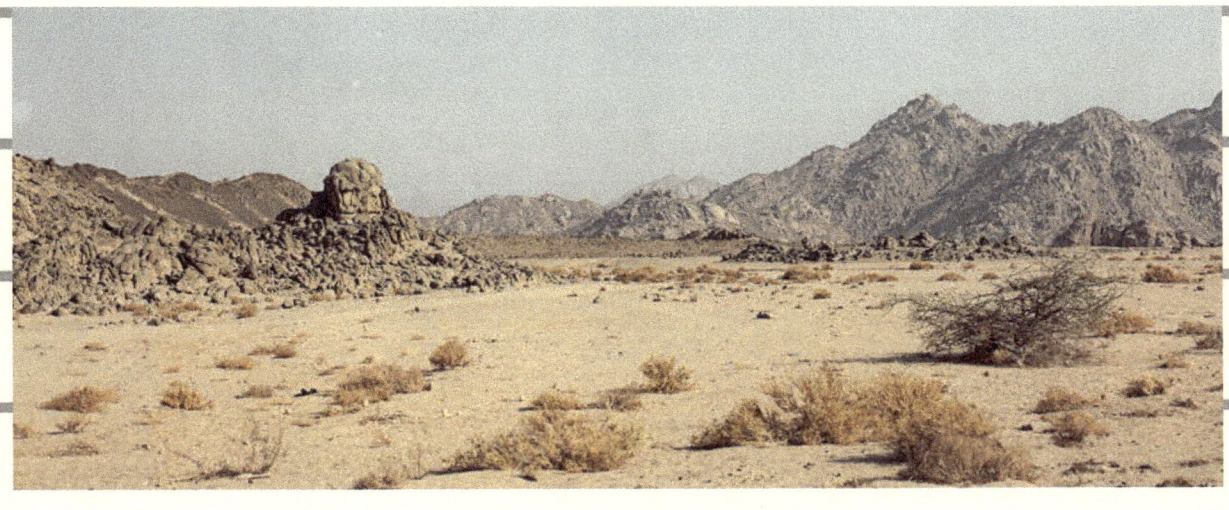

THERE ARE TREES AND STUFF
YEAH THIS PLACE IS PRETTY COOL
I LIKE THE VALLEY

# ELLIS

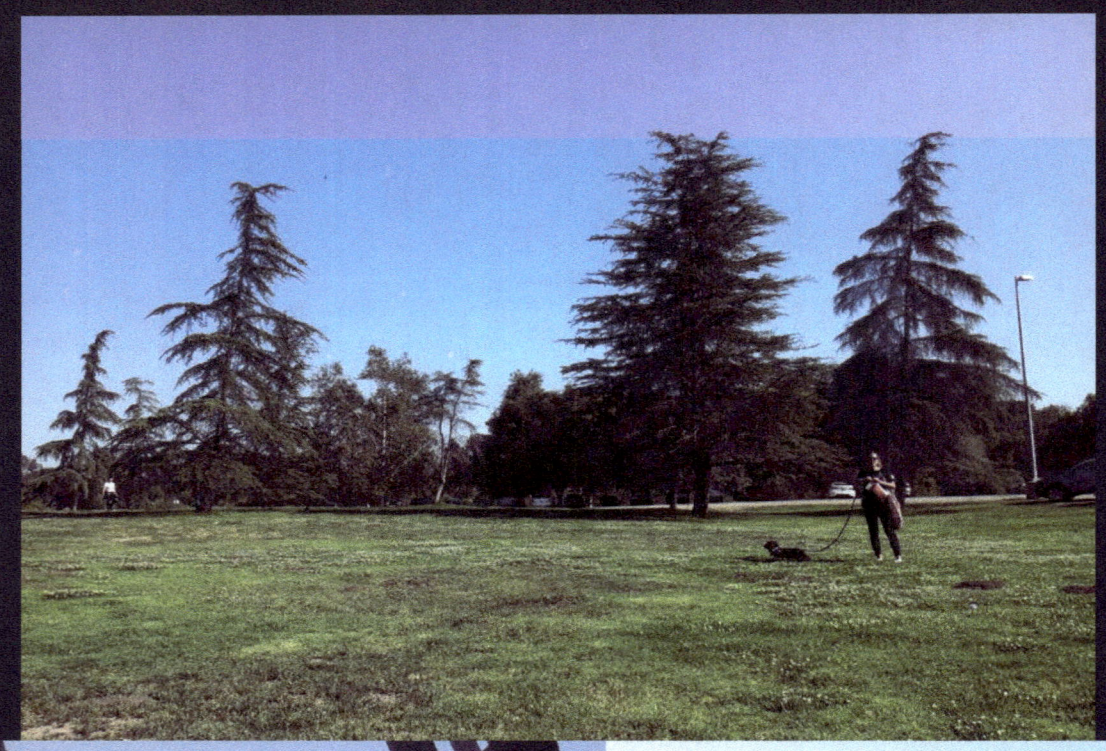

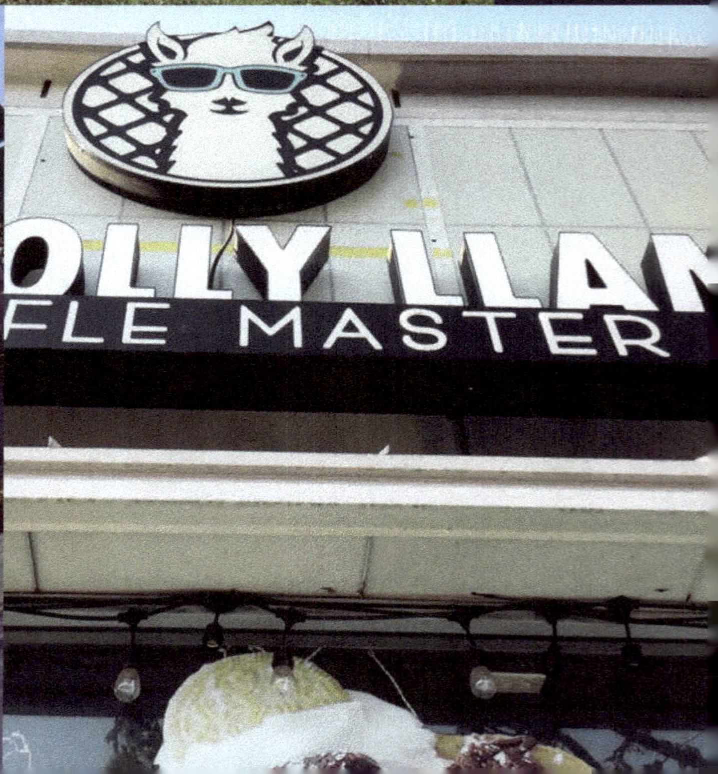

# ELLA

I smell salty air.
My dog barks at
the seagulls.
My feet burn on
sand.

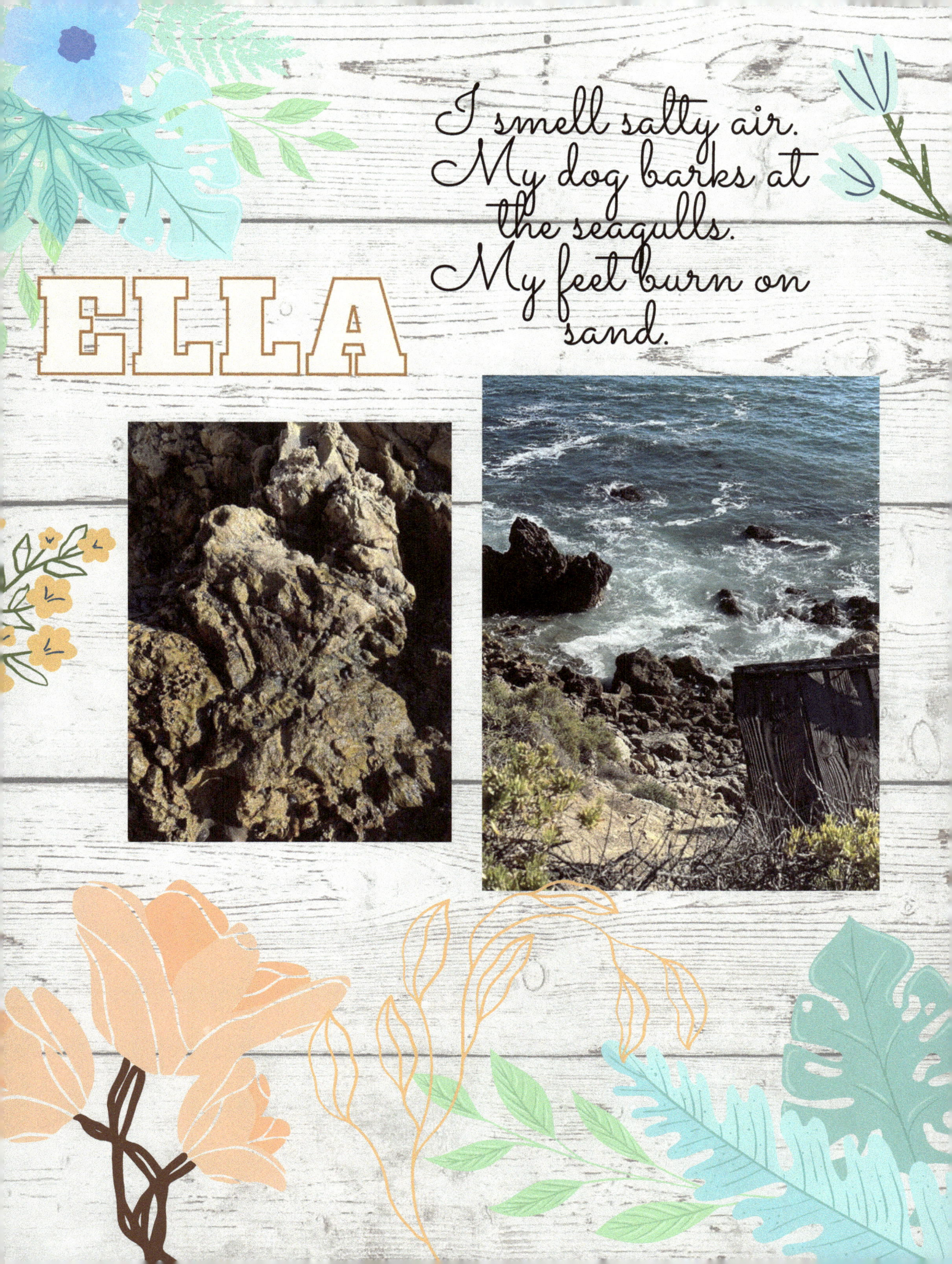

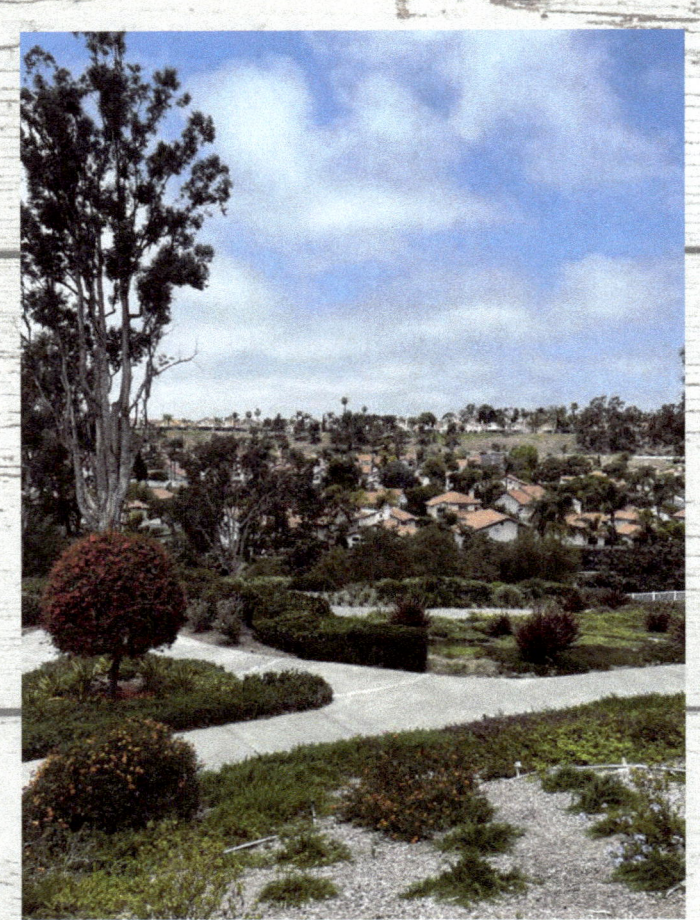

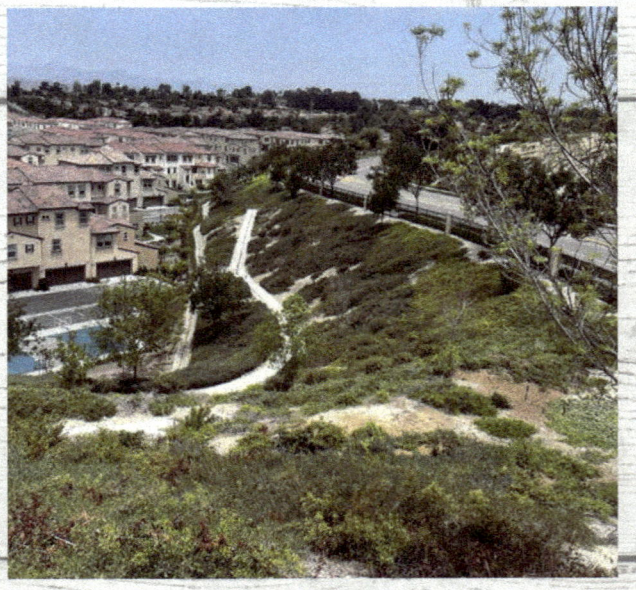

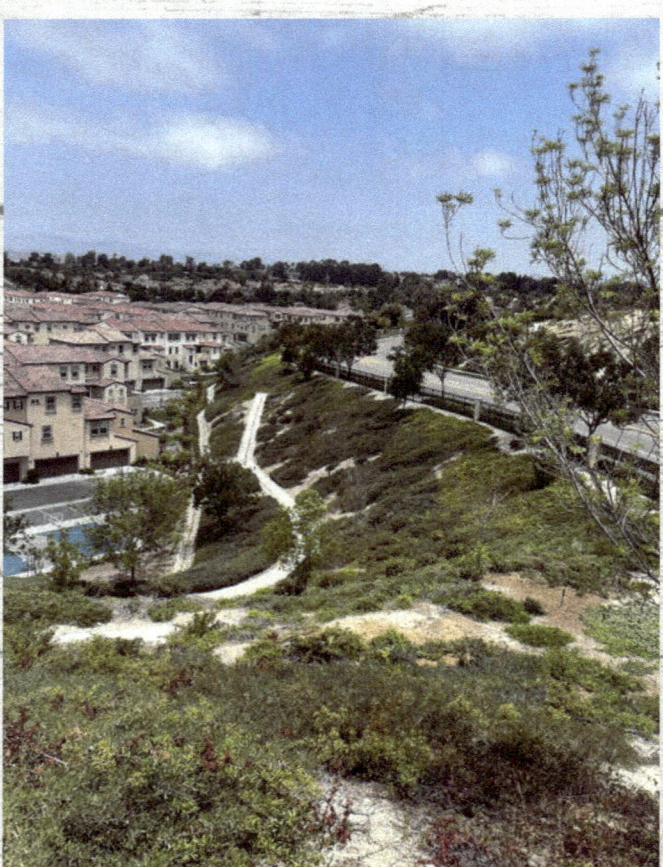

the sun is shining more than my led light
the birds are singing better than beyonce
the grass smells like poison ivy
the leaves are soft as a pillow.
the flowers are as beautiful as j lo.

**KAMRON**

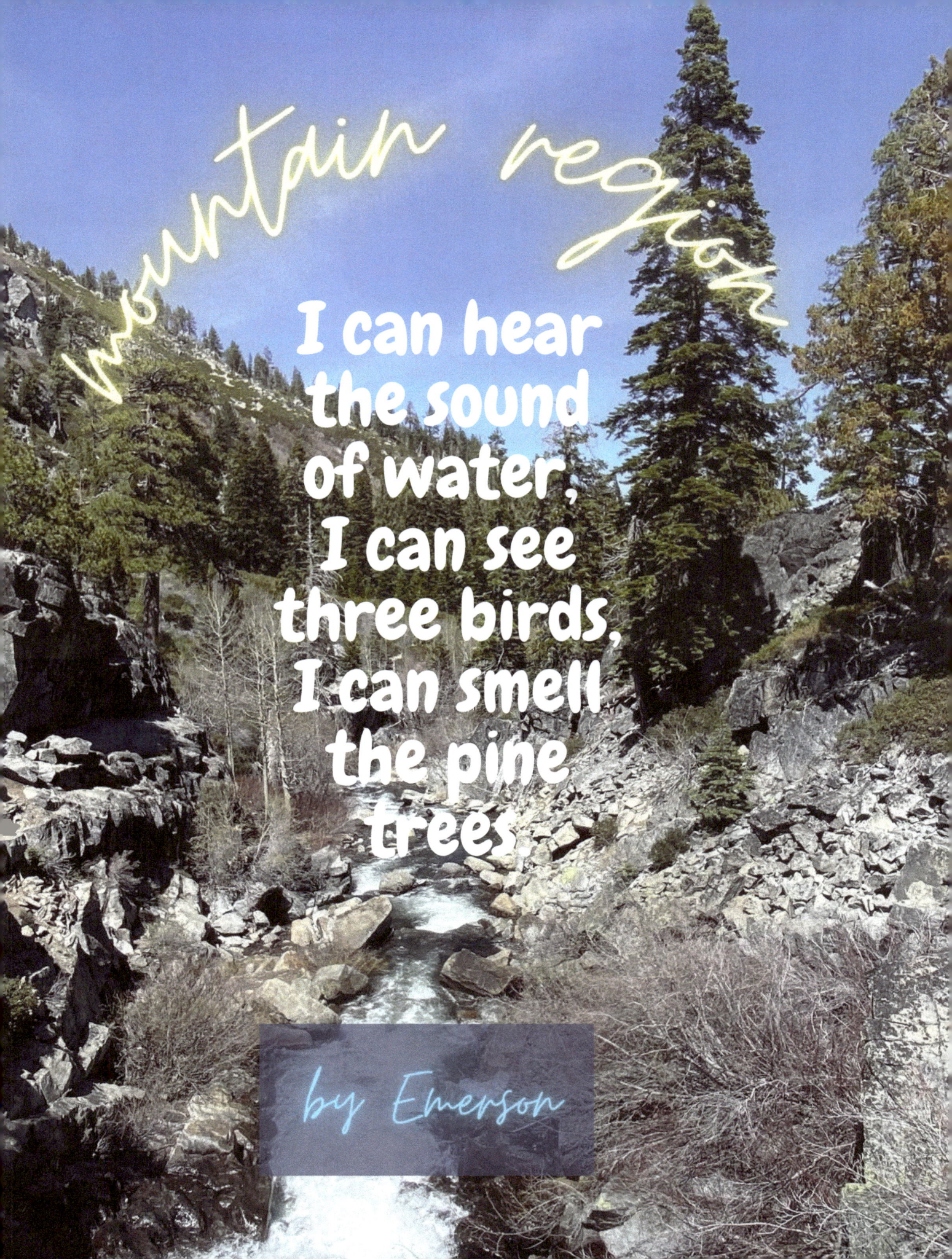

mountain region

I can hear the sound of water, I can see three birds, I can smell the pine trees

by Emerson

# mountain feel

the crisp
mountain
air
the fresh
mountain
sent and
the cold
smooth
rocks.
dear
Everett

# Tiny Starfish
## BY ISABELLE

TINY STARFISH, SMALL
IS HE TASTY, DON'T ASK ME
HAIRY LIKE DAD'S BEARD

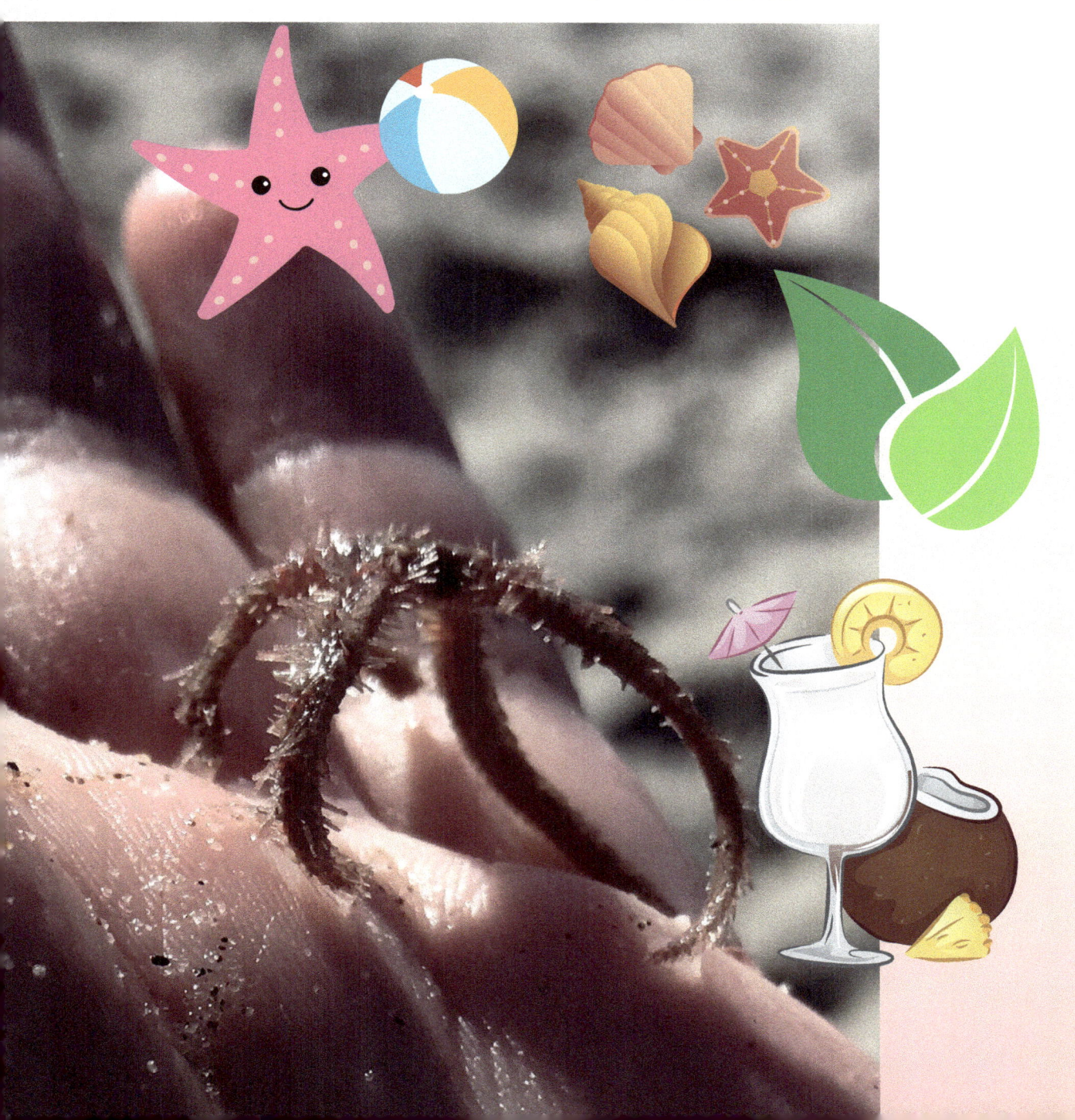

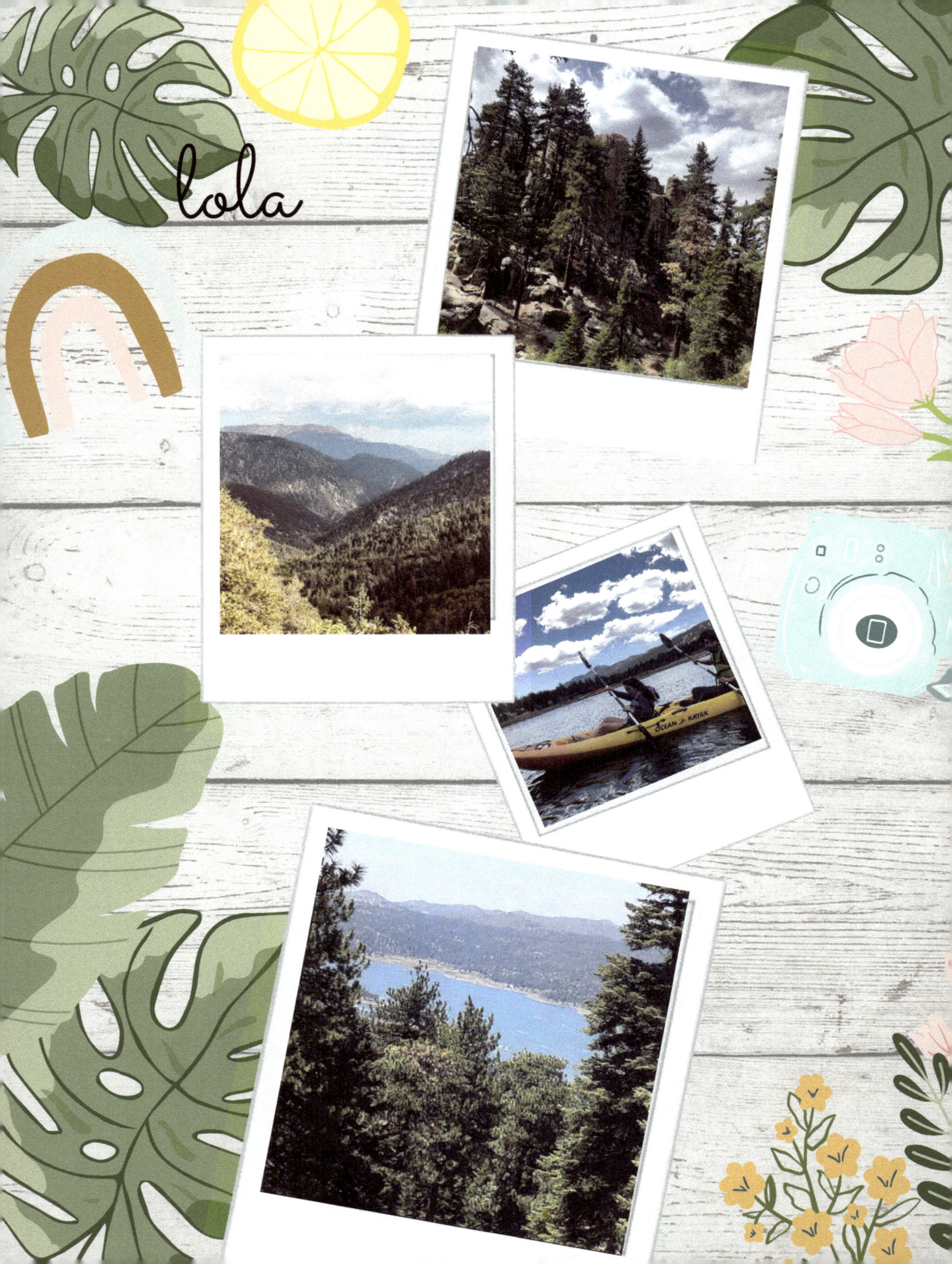

lola

# MAGNUS

the beautiful coast
waves crashing down on
the beach like a giant

stomp

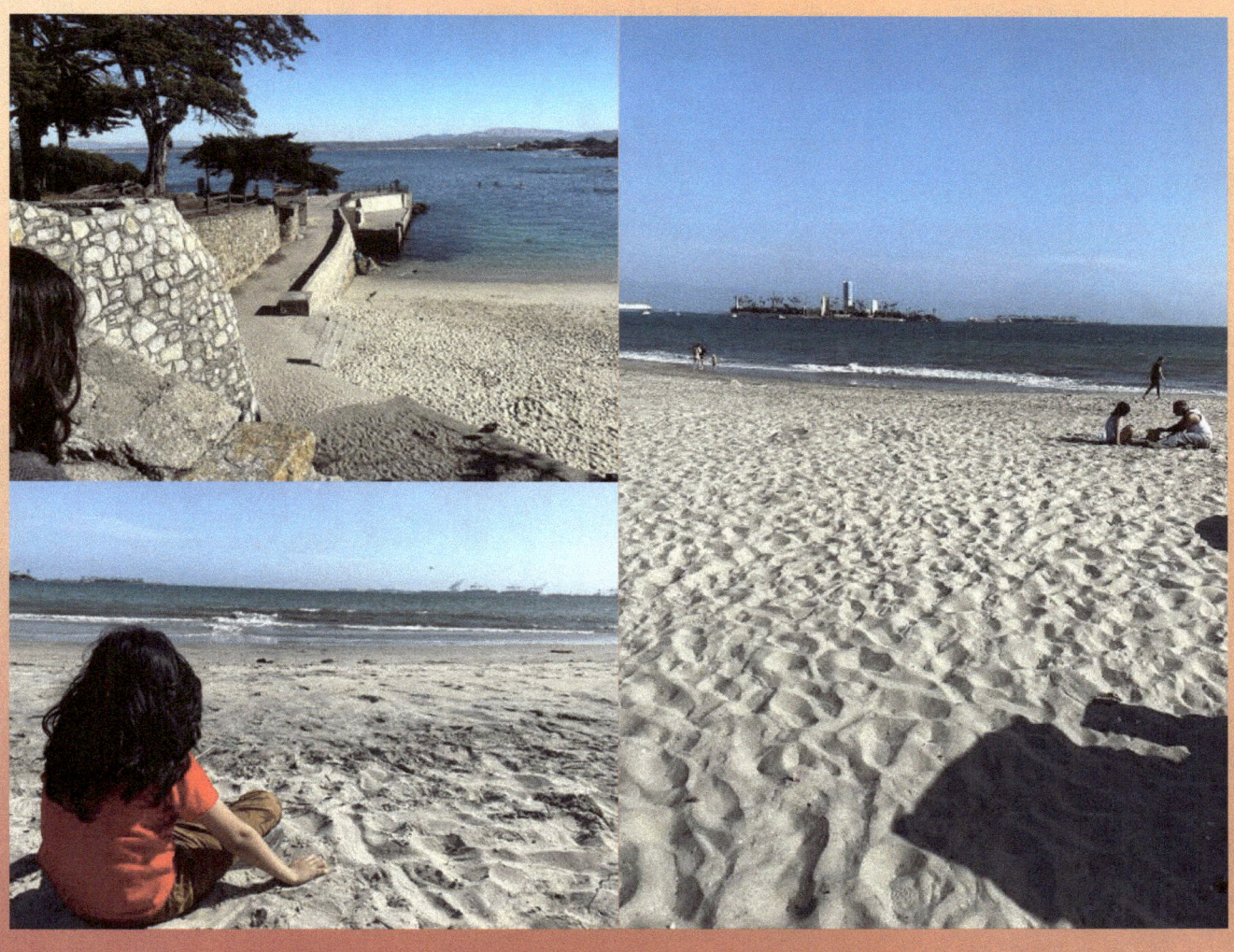

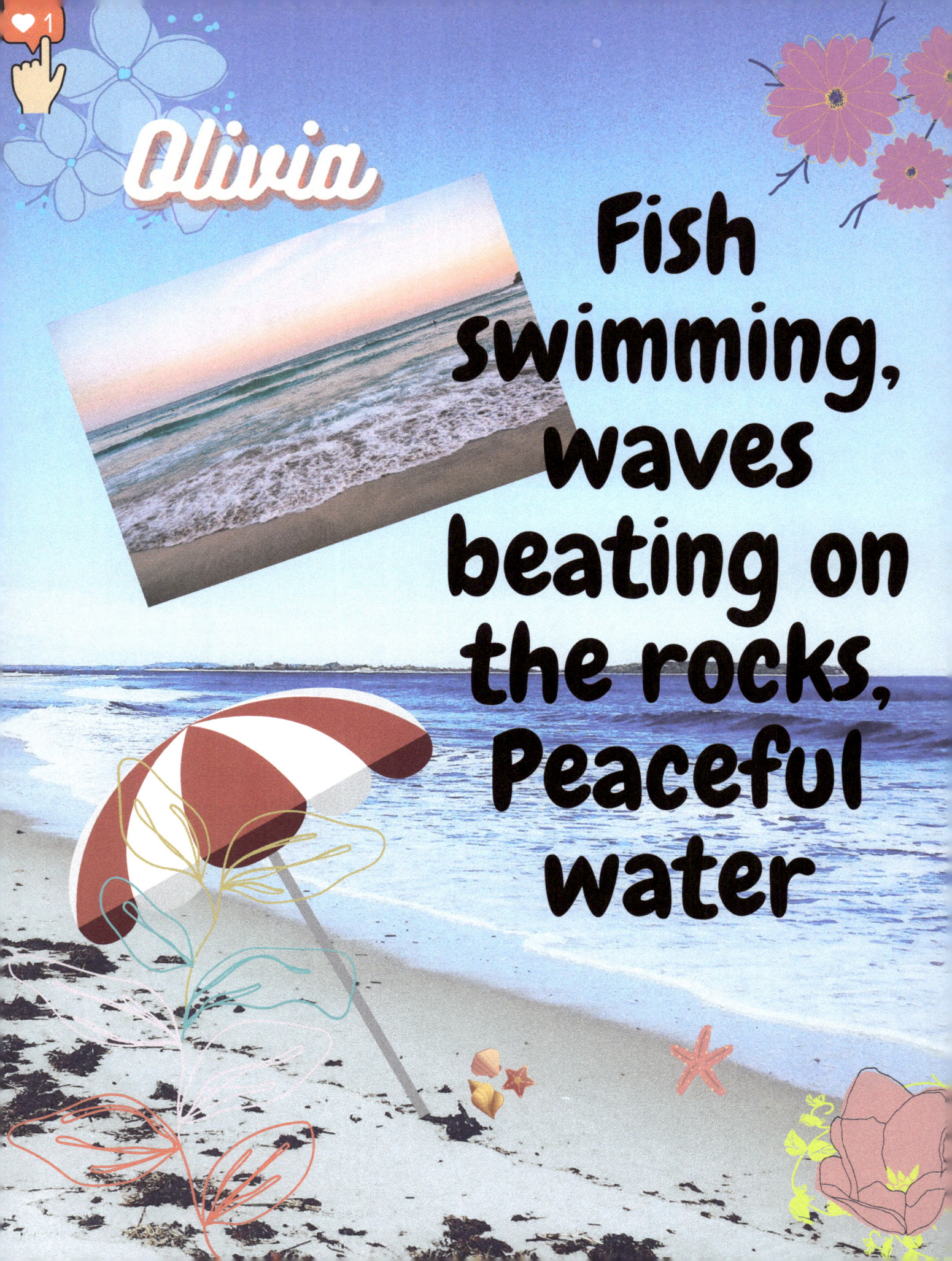

Olivia

Fish swimming, waves beating on the rocks, Peaceful water

# the sequoia trees

up in the mountains
majestic and strong
branches so high they can touch the sky
and a sweet smelling breeze
in the sequoia trees

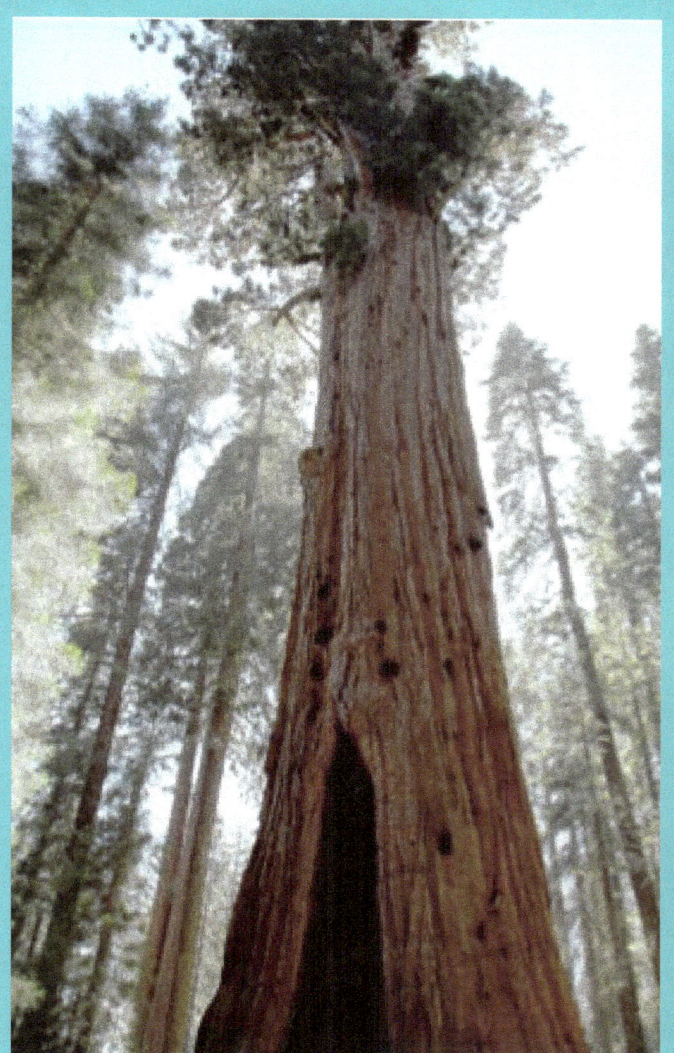
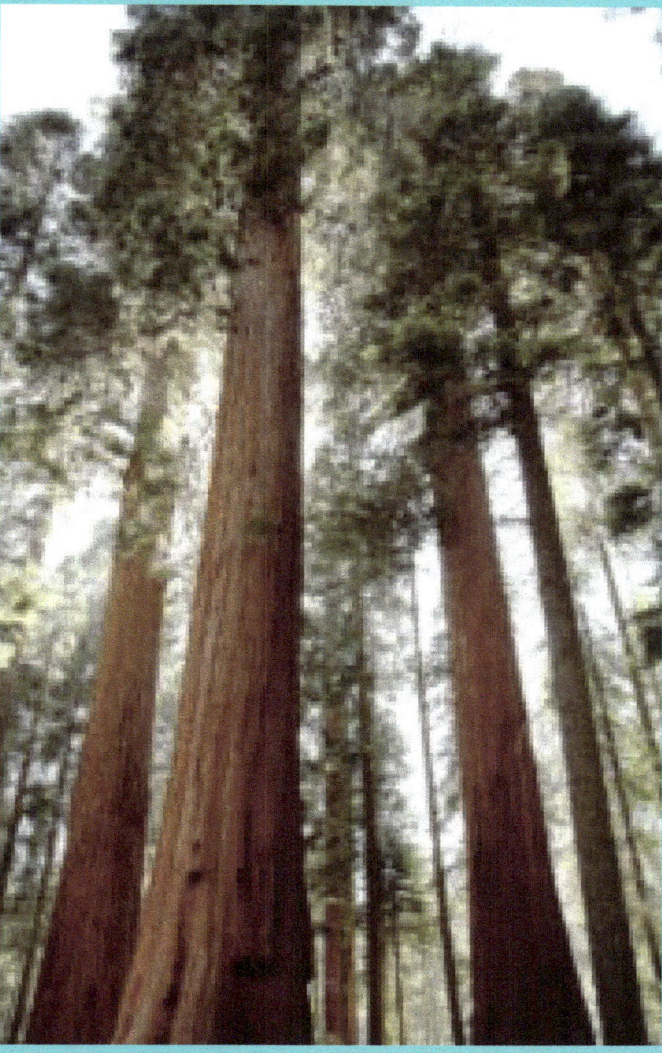

## Ophelia

# The Valley
## By Siena

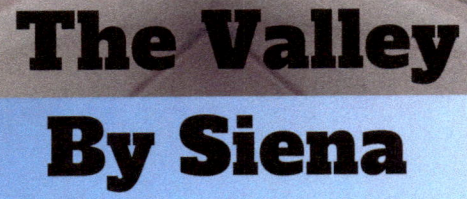

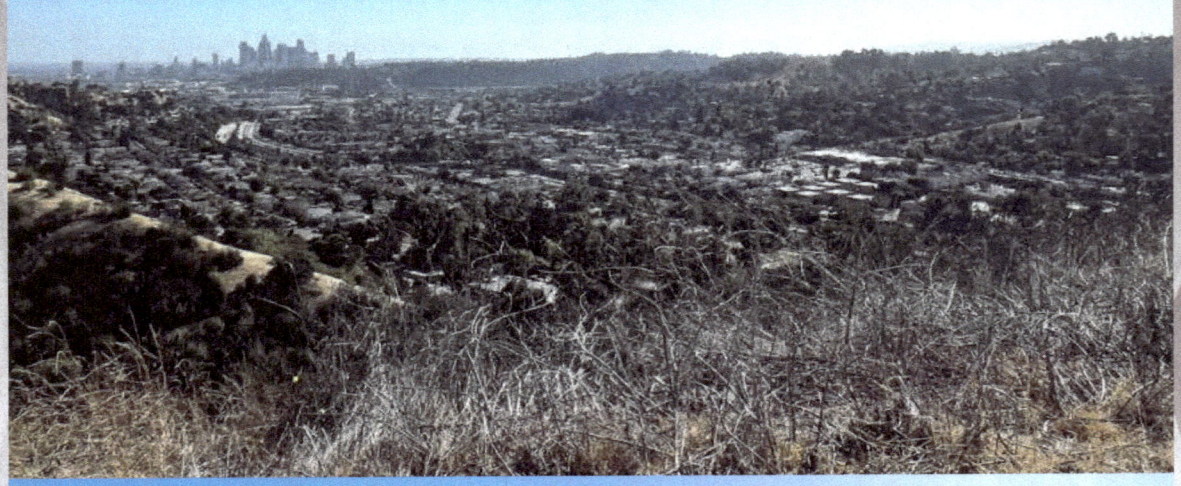

I FEEL SOMETHING FRESH

IS IT THE BIRDS OR THE HILLS?

IT IS THE VALLEY

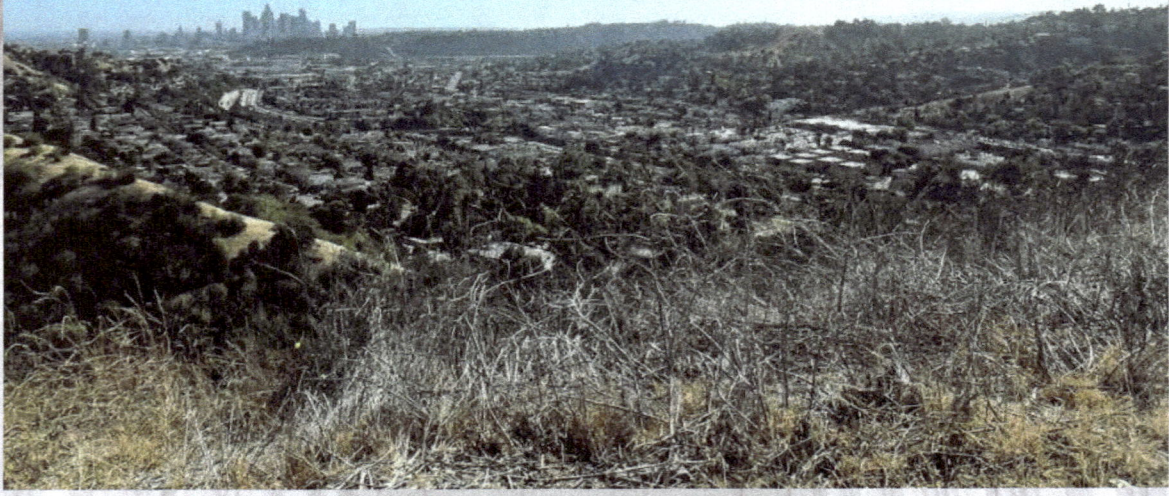

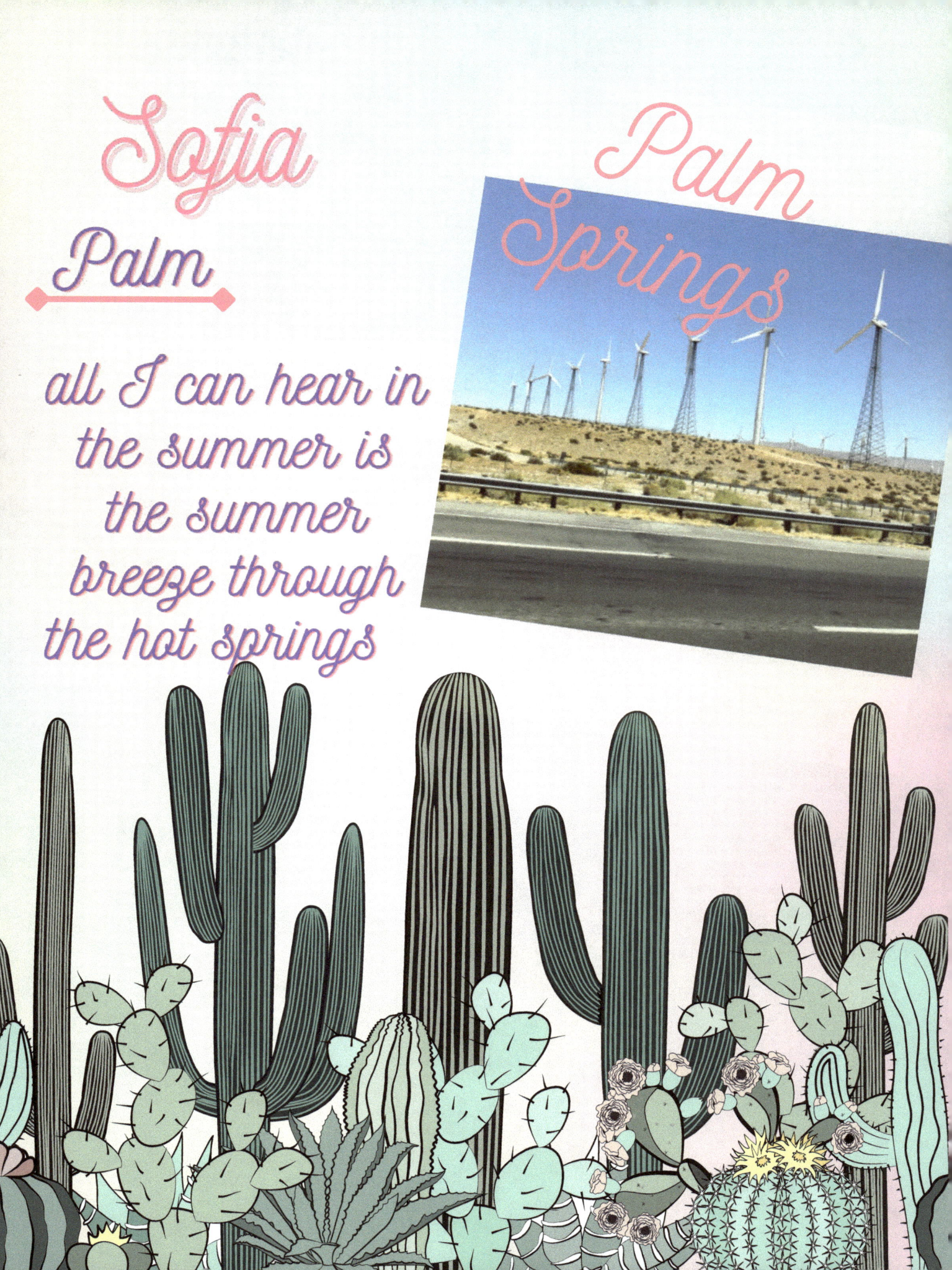

Sofia

Palm

all I can hear in the summer is the summer breeze through the hot springs

Palm Springs

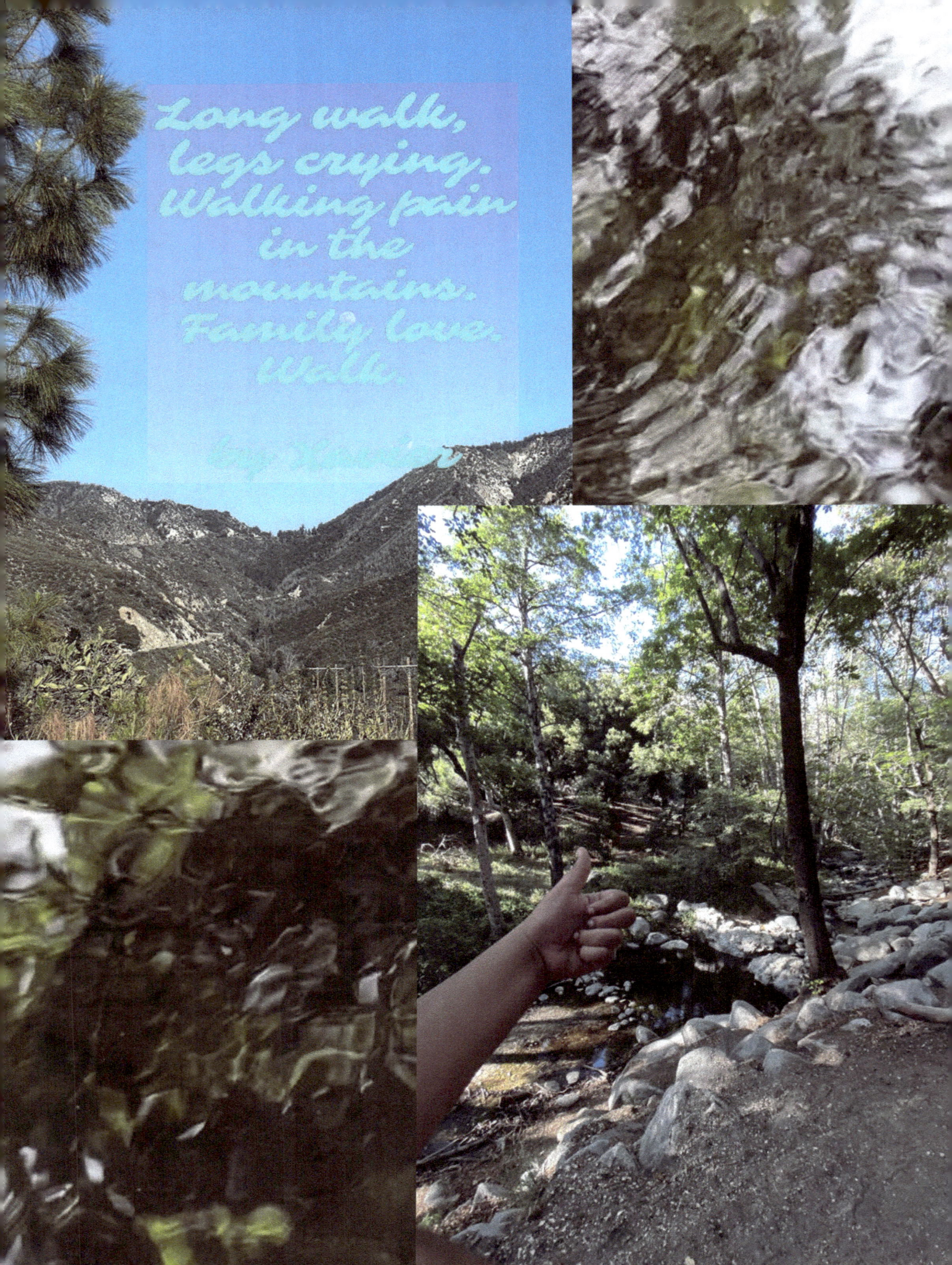

Long walk,
legs crying.
Walking pain
in the
mountains.
Family love.
Walk.